GUIDE TO
ECONOMIC INDICATORS

The Economist

GUIDE TO
ECONOMIC INDICATORS

Making Sense of Economics

C

CENTURY
BUSINESS

The
Economist
Books

First published in Great Britain in association with
The Economist Books by
Century Business, an imprint of Random Century Limited,
Random Century House,
20 Vauxhall Bridge Road,
London SW1V 2SA

Author Richard Stutely
Consultant Pam Woodall
Editor Penny Butler
Illustrations by The Economist Newspaper
Editorial Assistant Eleanor Martlew
Production Assistant Christine Campbell

Editorial Director Stephen Brough
Art Director Douglas Wilson
Production Manager Charles James

Any correspondence regarding this publication should be addressed to:
The Editorial Director, The Economist Books, Axe and Bottle Court,
70 Newcomen Street, London SE1 1YT

A catalogue record for this book is available from the British Library

ISBN 0-7126-9836-1

Printed and bound in Great Britain by
Butler & Tanner Ltd, Frome and London

CONTENTS

LIST OF TABLES

LIST OF FIGURES

Gross domestic product (GDP) and gross national product (GNP) are two very similar measures of total economic activity. GDP has slightly wider international usage and the term is used throughout this book to mean either GDP or GNP unless the context makes it clear that the reference is to one in particular. Precise definitions are given on page 25.

1

INTERPRETING ECONOMIC INDICATORS

"An economist is an expert who will know tomorrow why the things he predicted yesterday didn't happen today."
Dr Laurence J. Peter

All politicians seem able to demonstrate that their party presided over the fastest economic growth, the biggest fall in unemployment or the lowest inflation. Common sense suggests that they cannot all be correct. How can you interpret such claims?

This book shows how economic figures can be manipulated to demonstrate almost anything. More important, it explains how to read them, cut though any media hype and make up your mind about what they show, requiring no prior knowledge of economics or statistics. It deals with the 100 or so most important economic indicators, and answers questions such as the following.

- **What are they?** What is GDP, the invisibles balance, the terms of trade, the labour force?
- **What do they cover?** What is included in retail sales data, what is not in GDP, who is in the labour force?
- **What is their significance?** What do GDP, capacity use or the terms of trade tell us?
- **Where and when are they are published?** Should you look for weekly figures from the central bank, monthly information from a private organisation, quarterly numbers from the Department of Commerce, and so on.
- **How reliable are they?** Reasonably reliable in the case of spending by a particular government department, reasonably unreliable in the case of the size of the labour force. Who knows how many people not registered as unemployed would come forward if jobs were suddenly available?
- **Will they be revised, or are the first-reported figures set in stone?** For example, GDP data are revised endlessly, consumer-price data rarely.
- **How should they be interpreted?** The most important question.

Why interpret economic figures?

There are as many reasons for interpreting economic indicators as
there are published statistics. You may want to:

- get the best return on investing your money;
- measure companies and their products;
- judge if the time is right to give the go-ahead to a new capital
  investment project, to launch a takeover or to move into new
  markets;
- get a better understanding of how an economy is performing;
- judge the government's economic policies;
- obtain a feel for an unfamiliar economy;
- compare several countries;
- make a forecast; or
- simply obtain a better understanding of the news.

The countries

This book takes a global view and is intended as a guide to interpreting economic indicators worldwide.

Since it would be cumbersome if not impossible to list
figures for all countries, the tables generally show data for the
largest industrial countries, *The Economist 13*, which together
account for about 95% of industrial countries' output and 70% of
world output. Where appropriate, totals or averages are also
shown for the OECD and the European Community (see definitions below).

The same 13 countries form the basis for the economic and
financial indicators published in *The Economist* each week. This
book therefore provides the background to these figures and the
historical data behind the up-to-the-minute information.

America. If at times undue attention seems to be given to America, it is because the American economy occupies such a dominant
position, accounting as it does for over one-quarter of world output and over two-thirds of the output of the industrialised
countries.

Bankers, financiers and politicians worldwide depend on economic events in America. For example, apart from the direct
effects on the major financial markets, a change in the dollar's
exchange rate affects the prices of many internationally traded
commodities such as oil, and influences trade balances worldwide,
especially those of the 30 or so countries with currencies directly
pegged to the dollar.

Country groups. At the start of the 1990s total world economic output was over $20,000 billion a year. Table 1.1 shows how this was split among the industrial and developing countries, and various other groups which are sometimes used as a basis for analysis. The terminology and definitions are internationally accepted and are used by the World Bank (IBRD) and the International Monetary Fund (IMF), among others.

Table 1.1 **World output and trade**

	Countries no.	World GDP %	World exports %
Industrial countries			
USA	1	27.1	13.4
Japan	1	15.3	9.3
Germany	1	6.6	10.1
France	1	5.2	6.7
UK	1	4.4	7.5
Italy	1	4.6	4.4
Canada	1	2.7	3.4
Other industrial countries	16	10.5	19.1
Total industrial countries	23	76.2	73.9
Developing countries			
Africa	50	2.2	2.1
Asia	29	7.2	10.6
Europe	10	6.0	6.3
Middle East	15	2.6	3.7
Latin America & Caribbean	34	5.7	3.5
Total developing countries	138	23.8	26.2
Total world	161	100.0	100.0
Miscellaneous groups			
EC	12	25.9	39.8
Sub-Saharan Africa	45	0.8	0.7
Oil exporters	12	3.6	4.2
Dynamic Asian economies	4	1.9	6.6
Eastern Europe	6	1.6	2.2
Soviet republics	15	4.0	3.6

Note: Figures are 1990 estimates. The country groups are defined above except for the 12 oil exporters which are OPEC countries less Gabon and Ecuador (which have more diversified economies).

Source: World Bank

Developing countries and Africa. Of the 161 countries in Table 1.1, the 138 developing countries account for less than 25% of world output. Of these the 45 sub-Saharan African states account for less than 1% of world output. Many of them are debt-laden, with slow economic growth and low income per head. They are used in this book as an example of one of the extremes of economic performance.

3

Asia. At the other extreme, the four Asian newly industrialising countries (NICs) – Hong Kong, South Korea, Singapore and Taiwan – account for 2% of world output. Their rapid economic growth rates have been watched enviously by most other countries.

Key regional and economic groups

Group of Seven (G7)
Canada, France, Germany, Italy, Japan, the UK and the USA, which together accounted for two-thirds of world GDP at the start of the 1990s.

The Economist 13
The G7 plus Australia, Belgium, Holland, Spain, Sweden and Switzerland.

European Community (EC – 12 countries)
Belgium, Denmark, France, Germany, Greece, Holland, Ireland, Italy, Luxembourg, Portugal, Spain and the UK.

Industrial countries (23)
EC members plus Australia, Austria, Canada, Finland, Iceland, Japan, New Zealand, Norway, Sweden, Switzerland and the USA.

Organisation for Economic Co-operation and Development (OECD – 24)
The industrial countries plus Turkey. Yugoslavia has observer status but is not included in OECD totals for economic indicators.

Sub-Saharan Africa
African countries without a Mediterranean coastline.

Organisation of Petroleum Exporting Countries (OPEC – 14)
Algeria, Gabon, Ecuador, Indonesia, Iran, Iraq, Kuwait, Libya, Nigeria, Oman, Qatar, Saudi Arabia, United Arab Emirates and Venezuela.

Newly industrialising Asian economies (4)
Hong Kong, South Korea, Singapore and Taiwan.

Eastern Europe (6)
Bulgaria, Czechoslovakia, Hungary, Poland, Romania and Yugoslavia.

The term industrial countries is used in this book to refer to the OECD. Strictly speaking the two are not quite the same since the OECD includes Turkey, but the difference is negligible: Turkey accounts for well under 1% of OECD economic output. The republics of the former Soviet Union are identified in Table 1.3.

Figure 1.1

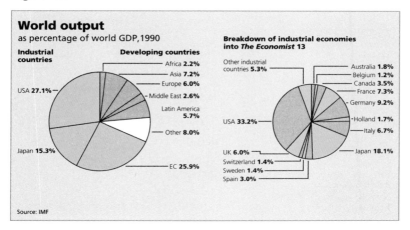

World output
as percentage of world GDP, 1990

Source: IMF

The indicators

This book groups the major economic indicators together in chapters to highlight linkages and aid interpretation. These groups, which are not mutually exclusive, cover the economy and economic growth, population and employment, government fiscal policies, consumers, investment and savings, industry and commerce, external flows, exchange rates, money and interest rates, and prices and wages.

The briefs. Each chapter begins with a short introduction followed by a series of briefs covering the key indicators. Each brief begins with a few lines summarising the indicator, its significance, what to look for, the source, and so on. These summaries, which are necessarily general, focus on what might be expected from a major industrialised country, such as America, Britain, Germany or Japan, when the economy is in relatively good shape.

Time periods. To aid interpretation, most of the tables show average rates of growth or another appropriate average for each of the past four economic cycles (see page 39). These cover a 30-year period and provide good yardsticks for judging future trends.

Germany. The former East and West Germanies unified on October 3rd 1990. Data for 1990 are dominated by western Germany and 1992 was expected to be the first year for which a wide range of consolidated figures would be produced. The data in Table 1.2 show the position for 1989, the last full year before unification.

Table 1.2   **Germany**

	West	East	United
Area ('000km²)	248.6	108.3	357.0
Population (m)	61.5	16.7	78.1
Employment (m)	27.8	8.6	36.4
% of total			
Agriculture	4.2	10.8	5.8
Mining & manufacturing	27.0	40.5	30.2
Construction	5.6	6.6	5.8
Services	41.0	40.1	40.8
GDP ($bn)	1189.1	159.4	1348.5
GDP per head ($)	19351	9560	17262
Visible trade ($bn)			
Exports	324.3	48.0	372.3
Imports	247.6	46.4	294.0
Trade balance	76.7	1.6	78.3
Visible trade (% of GDP)			
Exports	27.3	30.1	27.6
Imports	20.8	29.1	21.8
Trade balance	6.5	1.0	5.8
Sources: OECD; IMF; estimates			

Soviet republics. The break-up of the former USSR in 1991 increased the number of independent economies. Table 1.3 shows the relative size of the republics in 1988.

Table 1.3   **The former Soviet republics, 1988**

	Soviet republics' net output %	1987–89 World output %
Russia	61.1	2.44
Ukraine	16.2	0.65
Kazakhstan	4.3	0.17
Belarus	4.2	0.17
Uzbekistan	3.3	0.13
Azerbaijan	1.7	0.07
Georgia	1.6	0.06
Lithuania	1.4	0.06
Moldova	1.2	0.05
Latvia	1.1	0.04
Armenia	0.9	0.04
Tajikistan	0.8	0.03
Kyrgyzstan	0.8	0.03
Turkmenistan	0.8	0.03
Estonia	0.6	0.02
Total	100	4.00

Note: These figures are purely illustrative and should not be regarded as accurate to the number of decimal places shown.

Sources: IMF; World Bank

Sources of information

Countless economic figures are published every day in the news media and in various special reports, such as those circulated by investment advisers and financial institutions. The information is necessarily selective, and readers may wish to go back to the original source of the statistics.

National sources. Apart from the various trade organisations such as the US National Association of Purchasing Managers or the Confederation of British Industry (CBI), each country has its own sources of official statistics.

Sometimes the appropriate government department is self-evident; for example, labour statistics generally come from the department of employment or labour. For data which affect more than one department, such as GDP or balance of payments figures, good sources include the central bank or a central statistical agency, such as Germany's Federal Statistics Office or France's National Institute of Statistics and Economic Research (INSEE). In America the Commerce Department is the most comprehensive source of data.

Key statistical publications produced by official bodies in *The Economist 13* countries are listed below. In general central bank sources contain monetary data and the other sources cover more general figures, but there is usually some overlap between the two. These official sources frequently include a summary of the major private-sector figures. For example, Britain's *Economic Trends* reproduces some CBI data.

International sources. International organisations publish various national and international data, frequently in standardised or semi-standardised form, within a few weeks of their original release. Key sources include the following.

- **OECD.** The monthly *Main Economic Indicators* covers output, prices and trade in 24 industrialised countries. The numbers are often rebased (for example, to 1985=100), but are derived from the original national data. Periodic *Economic Surveys* and special reports provide data and analysis relating to economic developments in one member country or to one group of indicators such as employment data.

- **IMF.** The monthly *International Financial Statistics* covers monetary data and some other figures such as GDP and trade for the nearly 160 IMF member countries. Various special reports covering groups of indicators, such as exchange rates, are published occasionally.

- **UN (United Nations).** The *Monthly Bulletin of Statistics* includes some production and trade figures for a wide range of countries in more detail than IMF figures. Data on the production of various commodities are interesting.

- **European Commission.** The monthly *Eurostat* contains comparative data for EC member countries, while the quarterly *European Economy* includes statistics and ad hoc reports.

Useful national statistical publications

Australia
Reserve Bank: *Report and Financial Statement; Statistical Bulletin*
Australian Bureau of Statistics: *Monthly Review of Business Statistics; Digest of Current Economic Statistics*

Belgium
National Bank: *Annual Report; Bulletin*
National Institute of Statistics: *Bulletin of Statistics*

Canada
Bank of Canada: *Review*
Statistics Canada: *Canadian Statistical Review*

France
Bank of France: *Statistiques Monétaires Definitives; Statistiques Monétaires Provisoires; Quarterly Bulletin*
National Institute of Statistics and Economic Research (INSEE): *Monthly Statistics Bulletin; Informations Rapides*
Ministry of Economics, Finance and Budget: *Les Notes Bleues; Statistics and Financial Studies*

Germany
Bundesbank: *Monthly Report*
Federal Statistical Office: *Aussenhandel, Reihe 1, Wirtschaft und Statistik*

Holland
Netherlands Bank: *Annual Report; Quarterly Bulletin*
Central Bureau of Statistics: *Statistical Bulletin; Monthly Financial Statistics (Maandstatisteik Financiewezen); Sociale Maandstatisteik; Maandschrift (Monthly Bulletin)*

Italy
Bank of Italy: *Annual Report; Bulletin*
Central Institute of Statistics: *Monthly Bulletin*

Japan
Bank of Japan: *Economics Statistics Monthly*
Bureau of Statistics: *Monthly Statistics of Japan*

Spain
Bank of Spain: *Annual Report; Statistical Bulletin*
National Statistical Institute: *Monthly Bulletin of Statistics; National Accounts of Spain*

Sweden
Bank of Sweden: *Yearbook; Quarterly Review*
National Institute of Economic Research: *The Swedish Economy*
Central Bureau of Statistics: *Monthly Digest of Swedish Statistics; Statistical Reports*

Switzerland
> Swiss National Bank: *Annual Report; The Swiss Banking System; Monthly Bulletin*
> *Message of the Federal Council to the Federal Assembly*

UK
> Bank of England: *Quarterly Bulletin*
> Central Statistical Office: *Monthly Digest of Statistics; Economic Trends; Financial Statistics*

USA
> Board of Governors of the Federal Reserve System: *Federal Reserve Bulletin*
> US Department of Commerce: *Survey of Current Business*
> US Treasury Department: *Treasury Bulletin*

Interpretation

These are the first questions to ask when you come across any economic indicators.

- **Who produced the figures?** Was it a reliable government agency such as Statistics Canada or a recently established market research company?
- **Will the data be revised?** If so by how much? For example, the American retail sales figures for March 1991 first showed a 0.8% decline, but this was subsequently revised to a 0.7% rise.
- **To what period do the figures relate?** For example, American retail sales of $64 billion would be excellent for a month, appalling for a year.
- **Are the data seasonally adjusted?** If so is the adjustment reliable? For example, an increase in sales of umbrellas in the wettest month on record will not necessarily indicate a lasting improvement in the fortunes of umbrella companies.
- **What were the start and end points for changes?** For example, the change in unemployment between a recession and a boom will look much more impressive than the change between boom and slump.
- **What about inflation?** For example, a 5% increase in spending is rather disappointing if prices rose by 10% over the same period.
- **What other yardsticks will aid interpretation?** For example, total population, employment or GDP. A 5% rise in the number of jobs is not such good news if the working-age population expanded by 10% over the same period.

Chapter 2 runs through some critical ideas about numbers and their interpretation. Chapter 3 describes how economic activity is measured and comments on yardsticks and reliability. Chapters 4–13 cover the indicators themselves, as previewed above.

9

2

ESSENTIAL MECHANICS

*"Please find me a one-armed economist so we will not always
hear 'On the other hand ...'"*
Herbert Hoover, US president

This chapter looks at some basic methods of interpreting numbers
and some of the common associated problems. It also lays the
groundwork for analysing any kind of economic data.

Volume, value and price

When interpreting economic figures it is important to distinguish
between the effects of inflation and changes in the real level of
economic activity. Indicators measure one of three things:

- **volume**, such as tons of steel or barrels of oil;
- **value**, such as the market value of steel or oil produced in one
  month or year; or
- **price**, such as the market price of 1 ton of steel or 1 barrel of oil.

The relationship between these three is simple. *Volume* times *price*
equals *value* (see Table 2.1).

There is one possible complication. If the volume of oil or steel
produced each year is valued in the prices ruling in, say, 1985, the
result is an indicator of output in "1985 price terms". Such a
series is in money units, but it is a volume indicator because it
provides information about changes in volumes not prices. This is
known also as output in constant prices, real prices or real terms.

The value of steel output measured in actual selling prices is
known as a current price or nominal price series or a series in
nominal terms. Thus:

- **values, current prices, nominal prices and nominal terms**
  include the effects of inflation; while
- **volumes, constant prices, real prices and real terms**
  exclude any inflationary influences.

Table 2.1 OPEC crude oil production and prices

	volume	times	price	equals	value
	Production m barrels		Price $/barrel		Value of production $bn
1985	5913		27.45		162.3
1986	6643		15.04		99.9
1987	6533		17.90		116.9
1988	7283		14.84		108.1
1989	8030		17.44		140.0
1990	8577		22.18		190.2

Note: OPEC figures include Bahrain and Oman. The oil prices shown are OECD import prices.

Source: OECD

In Table 2.2 column A shows the money value of annual American economic output (gross domestic product or GDP, see page 25), which reflects changes in both output and prices. The next two columns disentangle these factors. Column B shows the volume of output with all goods and services measured in 1987 prices. Column C indicates the path of inflation (but see the comment on current-weighted index numbers below).

The value of output rose in 1981–82 (from $3,031 billion to $3,150 billion), yet in terms of the prices ruling in 1982, real output fell over the same period (from $3,843 billion to $3,760 billion).

Price indicators used to convert between current and constant prices (to deflate) are sometimes called price deflators.

- Current price series divided by constant price series ($\times$ 100) equals the price deflator.
- Current price series divided by price deflator ($\times$ 100) equals the constant price series.
- Constant price series times the price deflator ($\div$ 100) equals current price series.

Any series of numbers can be converted into index numbers, as described below for the current price series in Table 2.2 column D.

Step 1 A reference base is selected, 1987 in this case.
Step 2 The value in the reference base is divided by 100 (4,540 $\div$ 100 = 45.40).
Step 3 All numbers in the original series are divided by the result of step 2.

For example, the index value for 1981 is 3,031 $\div$ 45.40 = 67.

11

Table 2.2   **US GDP**

	Current prices $bn A	Constant 1987 prices $bn B	Price deflator index 1987=100 C	Current prices index 1987=100 D	Constant prices index 1987=100 E
1981	3031	3843	79	67	85
1982	3150	3760	84	69	83
1983	3405	3907	87	75	86
1984	3777	4148	91	83	91
1985	4039	4280	94	89	94
1986	4269	4404	97	94	97
1987	4540	4540	100	100	100
1988	4900	4719	104	108	104
1989	5244	4837	108	116	107
1990	5514	4885	113	121	108

Source: US Department of Commerce

Index numbers

Index numbers are values expressed as a percentage of a single base figure. For example, if annual production of a particular chemical rose by 35%, output in the second year was 135% of that in the first year. In index terms, output in the two years was 100 and 135 respectively.

Index numbers have no units. Chemical production in the second year is referred to as 135, not 135 tonnes or 135%. The advantages are that distracting units are avoided and changes are easier to assess by eye. The arithmetic is very straightforward, as shown in Table 2.2.

Composite indices and weighting. Frequently two or more indices are combined to form one composite index. For example, indices of consumer spending on food and on all other items might be combined into one index of total spending.

Base weighting. The most straightforward way of combining indices is to calculate a weighted average using the same weights throughout. This is known as a base-weighted index, or sometimes a Laspeyres index after the German economist who developed the first one. The following is an example of a base-weighted price index for single-person household consumption of wine and cheese each week.

Base data

Item	Price		Quantity consumed	
	1990	1995	1990	1995
Wine	9.00	10.50	5	6
Cheese	5.00	8.00	2	3

Where prices are in, say, Deutschemarks and quantities are litres of wine/kilos of cheese:

Weekly expenditure in 1990
= (1990 quantity of wine × 1990 price of wine)
+ (1990 quantity of cheese × 1990 price of cheese)
= (5 × 9.00) + (2 × 5.00)
= 45.00 + 10.00 = 55.00

Weekly expenditure in 1995, based on 1990 quantities
= (1990 quantity of wine × 1995 price of wine)
+ (1990 quantity of cheese × 1995 price of cheese)
= (5 × 10.50) + (2 × 8.00)
= 52.50 + 16.00 = 68.50

Index number for 1990 = 55.00/55.00 × 100 = 100.0
Index number for 1995 = 68.50/55.00 × 100 = 124.5

Current weighting. The problem with weighted averages is that weights usually need revising from time to time. With the consumer prices index, spending habits change because of variations in relative cost, quality, availability, and so on. One way to proceed is to calculate a new set of current weights at regular intervals, and use these to derive a single long-term index. This is known as a current-weighted index, or occasionally a Paasche index, again after its founder. The following is an example of a current-weighted price index for single-person household consumption of wine and cheese each week.

Base data

Item	Price		Quantity consumed	
	1990	1995	1990	1995
Wine	9.00	10.50	5	6
Cheese	5.00	8.00	2	3

13

Where prices are in, say, Deutschemarks and quantities are litres of wine/kilos of cheese:

Weekly expenditure in 1990, based on 1995 quantities
$$= (1995 \text{ quantity of wine} \times 1990 \text{ price of wine})$$
$$+ (1995 \text{ quantity of cheese} \times 1990 \text{ price of cheese})$$
$$= (6 \times 9.00) + (3 \times 5.00)$$
$$= 54.00 + 15.00 = 69.00$$

Weekly expenditure in 1995
$$= (1995 \text{ quantity of wine} \times 1995 \text{ price of wine})$$
$$+ (1995 \text{ quantity of cheese} \times 1995 \text{ price of cheese})$$
$$= (6 \times 10.50) + (3 \times 8.00)$$
$$= 63.00 + 24.00 = 87.00$$

Index number for 1990 = 69.00/69.00 $\times$ 100 = 100.0
Index number for 1995 = 87.00/69.00 $\times$ 100 = 126.1

Neither base weighting nor current weighting is perfect. Base-weighted indices are simple to calculate but they tend to overstate changes over time. Current-weighted indices are more complex to produce and they understate long-term changes.

Current-weighted price indices reflect changes in both prices and relative volumes, while base-weighted versions record price changes only. The price deflator in Table 2.2 is actually current-weighted (the US Commerce Department also produces a fixed-weighted price deflator, see page 184).

Mathematically, there is no ideal method for weighting indices; expediency usually rules. Most commonly indices are a combination of base-weighted and current-weighted. A new set of weights might be introduced every five years or so and the new index then spliced or chained to the old index. Table 2.3 shows how two indices are joined.

It is essential to know the basis for the weighting, as illustrated above.

Step 1 Identify one period when there are figures for both indices; 1988 in Table 2.3.
Step 2 For this period, divide the new figure by old figure; 83 ÷ 133 = 0.62.
Step 3 Multiply all old figures by the result; each figure in column C = figure in column A $\times$ 0.62.
Step 4 Put the rebased data with the new figures to create one long run of data.

Table 2.3 **Chaining index numbers**

	Old index A	New index B	Old index rebased C	Chained index D
1985	100		62	62
1986	110		69	69
1987	121		76	76
1988	133	83	83	83
1989		91		91
1990		100		100
1991		110		110

Effects of reweighting/out-of-date weights. To show the effects
of reweighting, consider GDP (total output) based on 1982 weights
when, say, manufacturing accounted for half of all economic
activity. If in 1990 manufacturing grew by 6% while all other
activity was static, initial 1990 figures showed total GDP rising by
6 × 0.50 = 3%. By 1992 the results of a major survey were available and GDP from 1988 was reweighted to take account of the
fact that the manufacturing sector had shrunk to a mere 10% of
total GDP. As a result the revised figure for total growth in 1990
was 6 × 0.10 = 0.6%.

This is obviously an extreme example, but index numbers can
easily become distorted if one item is much less or much more significant than the others. For example, demand tends to grow most
rapidly for goods and services which increase least in price, and so
on rebasing these items are allocated larger relative weights.

Figure 2.1

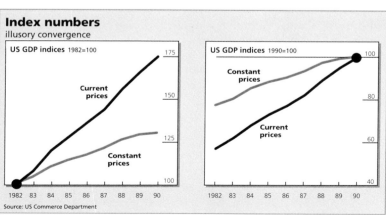

15

When looking at index numbers it is a good idea to check when they were last rebased and ask whether any component is increasing or decreasing in relative importance. The same approach should be taken to constant price series, such as the GDP data in 1982 dollars in Table 2.2, because these are essentially index numbers with a base value other than 100.

Convergence. Look out also for illusory convergence on the base. Two or more series will always meet at the base period because that is where they both equal 100 (see Figure 2.1). This can be highly misleading. When you encounter indices on a graph, the first thing to do is check where the base is located.

Measuring changes

If an index of stockmarket prices rose from 1,200 to 1,260, you could say either that it rose by 60 points or, alternatively, that it increased by 5%.

Stating the increase as 60 points (an absolute measure) is simple and straightforward. Yet to interpret the figure it must be judged against another figure, such as the starting level. A rise of 60 points in an index standing at 120 is much more dramatic than an increase of 60 points in an index which started at 12,000.

The percentage change (a relative measure) is easy to interpret. It indicates the size of a change when the starting level is 100. Percentages therefore provide a consistent yardstick for interpreting changes.

Calculating percentages. This is a matter of simple arithmetic. Basic rules for calculating percentage changes are given below. The various operations in the examples are very similar. They are designed to minimise the number of key strokes required when using a calculator. Multiplying or dividing by 100 and adding or subtracting 1 can be done by eye.

1 To find one number as a percentage of another.

	General procedure	Example 1	Example 2
	Y as % of X	150 as % of 120	120 as % of 150
Step 1	Divide Y by X	150 ÷ 120 = 1.25	120 ÷ 150 = 0.80
Step 2	Multiply by 100	1.25 × 100 = 125	0.80 × 100 = 80.0
		→150 is 125% of 120	→120 is 80% of 150

2 To find the percentage change between two amounts.

	General procedure	Example 1	Example 2
	Change between X and Y as % of X	change between 120 and 150 as % of 120	change between 150 and 120 as % of 150
Step 1	Divide Y by X	150 ÷ 120 = 1.25	120 ÷ 150 = 0.80
Step 2	Subtract 1	1.25 − 1 = 0.25	0.80 − 1 = −0.20
Step 3	Multiply by 100	0.25 × 100 = 25.0	-0.20 × 100 = −20.0
		→150 is 25% greater than 120	→120 is 20% smaller than 150

3 To find a given percentage of an amount.

	General procedure	Example 1	Example 2
	X% of Y	125% of 120	80% of 150
Step 1	Divide X by 100	125 ÷ 100 = 1.25	80 ÷ 100 = 0.8
Step 2	Multiply by Y	1.25 × 120 = 150	0.8 × 150 = 120
		→150 is 125% of 120	→120 is 80% of 150

4 To find an amount after a given percentage increase or decrease.

	General procedure	Example 1	Example 2
	Y increased by X%	120 increased by 25%	150 reduced by 20%
Step 1	Divide X by 100	25 ÷ 100 = 0.25	−20 ÷ 100 = −0.2
Step 2	Add 1	0.25 + 1 = 1.25	−0.2 + 1 = 0.8
Step 3	Multiply by Y	1.25 × 120 = 150	0.8 × 150 = 120
		→150 is 25% greater than 120	→120 is 20% less than 150

Basis points. Financiers deal in very small changes in interest or exchange rates. For convenience one unit, say 1% (that is, 1 percentage point) is often divided into **100 basis points**.

1 basis point	=	0.01 percentage point
10 basis points	=	0.10 percentage point
25 basis points	=	0.25 percentage point
100 basis points	=	1.00 percentage point

Common traps

Units and changes. Do not confuse percentage points with percentage changes. If an interest rate or inflation rate increases from 10% to 13%, it has risen by three units, or 3 percentage points, but the percentage increase is 30% (3 ÷ 10 × 100).

17

Up and back. A percentage increase followed by the same percentage decrease results in a figure below the starting level. For example, a 50% rise followed by a 50% cut leaves you 25% worse off.

* $1,000 increased by 50% is $1,500.
* 50% of $1,500 is $750.

Starting levels. A 10% pay rise for chief executives earning $500,000 a year puts an extra $50,000 in their annual pay packets. The same percentage increase for cleaners on $10,000 a year gives them a mere $1,000 extra.

The importance of the base from which changes are calculated is also illustrated in Tables 2.4 and 2.5.

Using Table 2.4, it could be claimed that in February 1992 the 12-month rate of inflation fell from 10% to 0%. In fact all that happened is that the increase a year earlier fell out of the 12-month comparison. In this example, shop prices changed just once during the period January 1989–February 1992, perhaps due to an increase in the rate of sales tax or VAT.

Table 2.4   **When did inflation fall?**

	Consumer prices index	% change over	
		1 month	12 months
1990			
January	100	0	0
February	100	0	0
1991			
January	100	0	0
February	110	10	10
March	110	0	10
1992			
January	110	0	10
February	110	0	0

Table 2.5 shows that UK engineering orders in the third quarter of 1990 were down from the previous quarter. However, the figure for the previous quarter was unusually high, and the third quarter figures were better than the first quarter's and any quarter of 1989. When comparing data over several years it is easy to overlook the distortion that can arise from using an unusually high or low starting or ending value.

Table 2.5 **Choosing the period for comparison**

	£bn	Over four quarters	% change From fourth quarter 1989 actual	annualised
1989				
1st quarter	33.3			
2nd quarter	33.8			
3rd quarter	34.3			
4th quarter	33.6			
Average for year	33.7			
1990				
1st quarter	34.3	3.0	2.1	8.6
2nd quarter	36.0	6.5	7.1	14.8
3rd quarter	35.2	2.6	4.8	6.4
4th quarter	32.9	−2.1	−2.1	−2.1
Average for year	34.6	2.7		

Source: UK Central Statistical Office

Growth rates

If consumer spending rises by 1% a month, by how much will it increase over a full year? Not 12%, but 12.7%. Each month expenditure is 1% greater than the month before and each percentage increase is calculated (compounded) from a higher base. Thus 12.7% a year is the same as 1% a month annualised. It is important to distinguish between the following terminology (numerical examples from Table 2.5).

- **12-month or 4-quarter change.** This compares one month or quarter with the same one in the previous year. For example, orders rose 2.6% between the third quarters of 1989 and 1990.
- **Change this year.** This compares the latest figure with the very end of the previous year. For example, when third quarter figures for 1990 were published, commentators might have said that orders had risen by 4.8% over the three quarters to the third quarter of 1990.
- **Annualised change.** This is the change which would occur if the movement observed in any period were to continue for exactly 12 months. For example, orders rose 6.4% annualised during the first three quarters of 1990.
- **Annual change.** This compares the total or average for one calendar or fiscal year with the previous one. For example, orders in 1990 were 2.7% higher than in 1989.
- **Change to end-year.** This compares end-year with end-year: e.g., orders fell by 2.1% over the four quarters to end-1990.

19

Table 2.6 Annualised and doubling rates

Observed % rate	Doubling time	Annualised rate if the observed rate is	
		quarterly	monthly
0.1	693.5	0.4	1.2
0.2	346.9	0.8	2.4
0.3	231.4	1.2	3.7
0.4	173.6	1.6	4.9
0.5	139.0	2.0	6.2
0.6	115.9	2.4	7.4
0.7	99.4	2.8	8.7
0.8	87.0	3.2	10.0
0.9	77.4	3.6	11.4
1.0	**69.7**	**4.1**	**12.7**
1.1	63.4	4.5	14.0
1.2	58.1	4.9	15.4
1.3	53.7	5.3	16.8
1.4	49.9	5.7	18.2
1.5	46.6	6.1	19.6
1.6	43.7	6.6	21.0
1.7	41.1	7.0	22.4
1.8	38.9	7.4	23.9
1.9	36.8	7.8	25.3
2.0	**35.0**	**8.2**	**26.8**
2.5	28.1	10.4	34.5
3.0	23.4	12.6	42.6
3.5	20.1	14.8	51.1
4.0	17.7	17.0	60.1
4.5	15.7	19.3	69.6
5.0	**14.2**	**21.6**	**79.6**
5.5	12.9	23.9	90.1
6.0	11.9	26.2	101.2
6.5	11.0	28.6	112.9
7.0	10.2	31.1	125.2
7.5	9.6	33.5	138.2
8.0	9.0	36.0	151.8
8.5	8.5	38.6	166.2
9.0	8.0	41.2	181.3
10.0	**7.3**	**46.4**	**213.8**
11.0	6.6	51.8	249.8
12.0	6.1	57.4	289.6
13.0	5.7	63.0	333.5
14.0	5.3	68.9	381.8
15.0	5.0	74.9	435.0
16.0	4.7	81.1	493.6
18.0	4.2	93.9	628.8
20.0	3.8	107.4	791.6

How to use Table 2.6. Locate in column 1 any observed rate, say a 1% monthly increase in consumer prices. If this rate continues, prices will double after almost 70 months (column 2) and increase by 12.7% in a year (final column). If the 1% change took place over one quarter (three months), the doubling time is 70 quarters (column 2) and the annual rate of increase is 4.1% (column 3).

Table 2.6 shows annualised rates for a selection of simple rates. American commentators tend to focus on annualised rates. This makes it easy to compare monthly or quarterly changes with perhaps more familiar annual rates, but it can be highly misleading. Many economic figures bump around from month to month, and annualised rates exaggerate erratic fluctuations. A mere 0.1% change in a month adds 1.2% to the annualised figure. Columns C and D of Table 2.7 compare simple and annualised changes and show how annualising can emphasise erratic fluctuations.

Each week the economic indicators pages of *The Economist* show changes in indicators such as industrial production and retail sales in two different ways: the percentage change over 12 months and the percentage change between the latest three months and the previous three months at an annual rate. The second measure is more susceptible to erratic short-term influences but it is useful for spotting whether economic activity is speeding up or slowing down.

The arithmetic for dealing with growth rates

1 To find the growth rate over several periods when the rate over one period is known.

	General procedure	Example 1	Example 2
	r% per period over n periods	0.3% per month for 12 months	7.5% per annum for 10 years
Step 1	Divide r by 100	$0.3 \div 100 = 0.003$	$7.5 \div 100 = 0.075$
Step 2	Add 1	$0.003 + 1 = 1.003$	$0.075 + 1 = 1.075$
Step 3	Raise to power of n	$1.003^{12} = 1.037$	$1.075^{10} = 2.061$
Step 4	Subtract 1	$1.037 - 1 = 0.037$	$2.061 - 1 = 1.061$
Step 5	Multiply by 100	$0.037 \times 100 = 3.7$	$1.061 \times 100 = 106.1$
		→Growth of 0.3% per month annualises to 3.7% a year	→Growth of 7.5% per year equals a 106.1% increase over 10 years

Note on step 3. Raising a number to the power of n is a shorthand way of saying multiply it by itself n times. For example, $2^3 = 2 \times 2 \times 2 = 8$. Use the calculator key marked xy (the letters might be slightly different) to perform this operation. If there is no xy key use logarithms (the LOG and 10x or LN and ex keys).

Replace step 3 with the following.

Step 3a	Take the log	Log 1.003 = 0.0013	Log 1.075 = 0.0314
Step 3b	Multiply by n	0.0013 × 12 = 0.0156	0.0314 × 10 = 0.314
Step 3c	Take the antilog	Antilog 0.0156 = 1.037	Antilog 0.314 = 2.061

The formula for these calculations is $[(1 + r/_{100})^n - 1] \times 100$ or, for PC spreadsheet users, $(EXP(LN(1 + r/100)*n) - 1)*100$.

2 To find the growth rate over one period when the rate over several periods is known.

	General procedure	Example 1	Example 2
	r% over n periods	3.7% over 12 months	106.1% over 10 years
Step 1	Divide r by 100	3.7 ÷ 100 = 0.037	106.1 ÷ 100 = 1.061
Step 2	Add 1	0.037 + 1 = 1.037	1.061 + 1 = 2.061
Step 3	Raise to power of 1/n	$1.037^{1/12} = 1.003$	$2.061^{1/10} = 1.075$
Step 4	Subtract 1	1.003 − 1 = 0.003	1.075 − 1 = 0.075
Step 5	Multiply by 100	0.003 × 100 = 0.3	0.075 × 100 = 7.5
		→Growth of 3.7% per annum equals 0.3% per month	→Growth of 106.1% over 10 years equals 7.5% per annum

Note on step 3. If your calculator does not have an $x^{1/y}$ key, use logarithms (the LOG and 10x or LN and ex keys). Replace step 3 with the following.

Step 3a	Take the log	Log 1.037 = 0.0156	Log 2.061 = 0.314
Step 3b	Divide by n	0.0156 ÷ 12 = 0.0013	0.314 ÷ 10 = 0.0314
Step 3c	Take the antilog	Antilog 0.0013 = 1.003	Antilog 0.0314 = 1.075

The formula for these calculations is $[(1 + r/_{100})^{1/n} - 1] \times 100$ or, for PC spreadsheet users, $(EXP(LN(1 + r/100)/n) - 1)*100$.

Moving averages

One way to smooth out erratic fluctuations is to look at an average. When reviewing, say, total high street sales in June, you might take an average of figures for May, June and July. A sequence of such averages is called a moving average. Column E of Table 2.7 and the footnote show the calculation of a three-month moving average for a short run of data.

The moving average can average any number of periods. A five-year moving average helps to smooth out the economic cycle described on pages 51–55, although a lot of data would be needed to calculate it. Moreover, the more periods covered by a moving average, the slower it will be to show changes in trend.

Seasonality

Most economic figures show a seasonal pattern that repeats itself every year. For example, prices of seasonal foods rise in the winter, sales of beachwear increase with the onset of summer, and industrial production falls in the months when factories close for annual holidays.

Seasonal adjustment. There is a simple numerical process called seasonal adjustment which adjusts raw data for the observed seasonal pattern (described in detail in *The Economist Numbers Guide*). Briefly, if sales or output in February are typically 85% of the monthly average, the seasonal adjustment process divides all observations for February by 85%.

Many published figures are seasonally adjusted to aid interpretation, but it is important to remember that seasonal adjustment is not infallible. For example, in a particularly cold month energy use increases by more than the amount expected by seasonal adjustment, while more building workers than usual are temporarily laid off. The adjusted figures might be erroneously taken to suggest that energy use or unemployment was rising when the underlying situation was very different. Climatic and other influences might be overlooked when viewing the economy from the comfort of seasonally adjusted data.

Coping with seasonality and blips. Table 2.7 indicates some problems of interpreting data which are subject to erratic or seasonal influences.

- The figures in column A are an index of retail sales. At first glance it appears that sales in January 1992 were very poor, since there was a 4% decline from the previous month (column B). It seems that this interpretation is confirmed because the 4% fall is worse than the 0.2% decline in the same month a year earlier.
- The percentage changes over 12 months (column D) give some encouragement. They indicate that the trend in sales is upward, though growth over the 12 months to January 1992 (6.2%) was slacker than in the previous few months (around 10%).
- Column F smooths out short-term erratic influences by comparing sales in the latest three months with sales in the same three months a year earlier. This suggests that the fall in January was not as severe as it appeared at first glance, with the 12-month growth rate remaining at close to 10%.

This final interpretation is the correct one. Indeed, a full run of figures would show that sales fell in January only because this was a correction to an exceptionally steep rise in the earlier few months.

Table 2.7   **Analysing seasonal and erratic influences**

	Retail sales index	% change over			3-month moving average	
		1 month	1 month annualised	12 months	Index	% change from 12 months ago
	A	B	C	D	E	F
1990						
Oct	119.2					
Nov	120.2	0.8				
Dec	121.8	1.3			120.4	
1991						
Jan	121.6	−0.2			121.2	
Oct	130.7	−0.5	−5.8	9.6		
Nov	133.4	2.1	27.8	11.0		
Dec	134.4	0.7	9.3	10.3	132.8	10.3
1992						
Jan	129.2	−3.9	−37.7	6.2	132.3	9.2

Note: Calculations for January 1992:
Column B: $[(129.2 \div 134.4) - 1] \times 100 = -3.9\%$
Column C: $[(129.2 \div 134.4)^{12} - 1] \times 100 = -37.7\%$
Column D: $[(129.2 \div 121.6) - 1] \times 100 = 6.2\%$
Column E: $(133.4 + 134.4 + 129.2) \div 3 = 132.3$
Column F: $[(132.3 \div 121.2) - 1] \times 100 = 9.2\%$

Commentators are inclined to interpret blips as changes in trend. In general you should examine a run of data, form a view about the trend, and stick to it until there is clear evidence that the trend has changed.

3

MEASURING ECONOMIC ACTIVITY

"GDP should really stand for grossly deceptive product."
The Economist

Total economic activity may be measured in three different but equivalent ways.

Perhaps the most obvious approach is to add up the value of all goods and services produced in a given period of time, such as one year. Money values may be imputed for services such as health care which do not change hands for cash. Since the output of one business (for example, steel) can be the input of another (for example, automobiles), double counting is avoided by combining only "value added", which for any one activity is the total value of production less the cost of inputs such as raw materials and components valued elsewhere.

A second approach is to add up the expenditure which takes place when the output is sold. Since all spending is received as incomes, a third alternative is to value producers' incomes.

Thus output = expenditure = incomes.

The precise definition of economic activity varies. The three main concepts are gross domestic product, gross national product and net national product.

Gross domestic product. GDP is the total of all economic activity in one country, regardless of who owns the productive assets. For example, Britain's GDP includes the profits of a foreign firm located in Britain even if they are remitted to the firm's parent company in another country.

Gross national product. GNP is the total of incomes earned by residents of a country, regardless of where the assets are located. For example, Britain's GNP includes profits from British-owned businesses located in other countries.

Net national product. The "gross" in GDP and GNP indicates that there is no allowance for depreciation (capital consumption), the amount of capital resources used up in the production process due to wear and tear, accidental damage, obsolescence or retirement of capital assets. Net national product is GNP less depreciation.

The relationship between the three measures is straightforward:

GDP (gross domestic product)
+ net property income from abroad (rent, interest, profits and dividends)
= GNP (gross national product)
– capital consumption (depreciation)
= NNP (net national product)

Capital consumption. Capital consumption is not identifiable from a set of transactions; it can only be imputed by a system of conventions. For example, when investment spending of $1m on a new machine is included in GDP figures, national accounts statisticians pencil in depreciation of, say, $100,000 a year for each of the next ten years. This gives a stinted view of productive capacity. After five years the machine might still be producing at full capacity, but the national accounts would show it as capable of producing only half the volume that it could when new.

Choosing between GDP, GNP and NNP

Net national product (NNP) is the most comprehensive measure of economic activity, but it is of little practical value due to the problems of accounting for depreciation. Gross concepts are more useful.

Analysts tend to say that GDP is a better measure than GNP, although in practice the choice between the two depends largely on national conventions. Of the major industrial countries, only Germany and Japan focus on GNP, all the rest prefer GDP. (America used GNP until the end of 1991.) The difference between GDP and GNP is usually relatively small, perhaps 1% of GDP, but there are a few exceptions; for example, in 1989 Kuwait's GNP was 35% bigger than its GDP, due to the country's vast income from foreign assets. In the short term a large change in total net property income has only a minor effect on GDP. When reviewing longer-term trends, it is advisable to check net property income to see if it is making GNP grow faster than GDP.

Net material product

Some countries, mainly centrally planned economies, use or have used net material product (NMP) to measure overall economic activity. This will probably be supplanted by GDP in the former communist countries which adopt market economies in the 1990s. NMP is less comprehensive than GDP because it excludes "non-productive services", such as banking, government administration, health and education, and is quoted net of capital consumption (depreciation). As a rule of thumb, NMP is roughly 80–90% of GDP.

> Did the American economy start to recover in the second quarter of this year [1991], or was it stuck in recession? America's real gross national product (GNP), the measure that is watched by the government and Wall Street and splashed across newspaper headlines, fell by 0.1% at an annual rate in the second quarter. However, gross domestic product (GDP) rose by 0.8% at an annual rate. By coincidence, the Department of Commerce has just decided that from November [1991], when the third-quarter figures will be released, it will concentrate more on GDP than on GNP.
>
> Cynics might claim that the switch to GDP is a bid to fiddle the figures. In fact it is America's first step to bring its national accounts into line with most of the rest of the world.
>
> GNP is probably more useful in comparing the relative levels of income per head in different countries, but GDP provides a better guide to changes in domestic production – and hence is the better tool for steering economic policy. Because net income from abroad tends to be volatile, the two measures can often move in completely different directions from one quarter to another. Over longer periods, however, the two measures usually fall into step. Indeed, since the third quarter of last year [1990], America's GDP and GNP have both fallen by exactly the same amount. The government cannot boost its flagging growth rate simply by revising its figures; that requires a revision of its policies.
>
> *The Economist*, September 21st 1991

OMISSIONS

Deliberate omissions

There are many things which are not in GDP, including the following.
- **Transfer payments.** For example, social security and pensions.
- **Gifts.** For example, $10 from Aunt Agatha on your birthday.
- **Unpaid and domestic activities.** If you cut your grass or

paint your house the value of this productive activity is not recorded in GDP, but it is if you pay someone to do it for you.

- **Barter transactions**. For example, the exchange of a sack of wheat for a can of petrol.
- **Second-hand transactions**. For example, the sale of a used car (where the production was recorded in an earlier year).
- **Intermediate transactions**. For example, a lump of metal may be sold several times, perhaps as ore, pig iron, part of a component and, finally, part of a washing machine (the metal is included in GDP once at the net total of the value added between the initial production of the ore and its final sale as a finished item).
- **Leisure**. An improved production process which creates the same output but gives more recreational time is recorded in the national accounts at exactly the same value as the old process.
- **Depletion of resources**. For example, oil production is recorded at sale price minus production costs and no allowance is made for the fact that an irreplaceable part of the nation's capital stock of resources has been consumed.
- **Environmental costs**. GDP figures do not distinguish between green and polluting industries.
- **Allowance for non-profit making and inefficient activities.** The civil service and police force are valued according to expenditure on salaries, equipment, and so on (the appropriate price for these services might be judged to be very different if they were provided by private companies).
- **Allowance for changes in quality.** You can buy very different electrical goods for the same inflation-adjusted outlay as a few years ago, but GDP data do not take account of such technological improvements.

Some of the exclusions can be identified elsewhere. For example, environmental costs are seen in statistics on pollution and most countries report known oil or coal reserves (although these estimates may be over-optimistic or clouded by genuine ignorance about the size of underground reserves).

One other point to note is that the more advanced government statistical agencies include in GDP an allowance for the imputed rent paid by home owner-occupiers. This avoids an apparent change in national output because of any switch between owner-occupation and renting.

Surveys and sampling

Many of the figures which go into GDP are collected by surveys. For example, governments ask selected manufacturing or retailing companies for details of their output or sales each month. This information is used to make inferences about all manufacturers or all retailers. Such estimates may not be correct, especially as the most dynamic parts of the economy are small firms constantly coming into and going out of existence, which may never be surveyed.

Sample evidence is supplemented by other information, including documentation required initially for bureaucratic purposes such as customs clearance or tax assessment. Such data take a long time to collect and analyse, which is why economic figures are frequently revised even when they are several years old.

Unrecorded transactions

GDP may under-record economic activity, not least because of the difficulties of keeping track of new small businesses and because of tax avoidance or evasion.

Deliberately concealed transactions form the black, hidden or shadow economy. This is largest at times when, and in countries where, taxes are high and bureaucracy is smothering. Estimates of the size of the shadow economy vary enormously. For example, differing studies put America's at 4–33%, Germany's at 3–28% and Britain's at 2–15%. What is agreed, though, is that among the industrial countries the black economy is largest in Italy, at perhaps one-third of GDP, followed by Spain, Belgium and Sweden, while the smallest black economies are in Japan and Switzerland at around 4% of GDP.

The only industrial countries that adjust their GDP figures for the shadow economy are Italy and America and they may well underestimate its size.

OUTPUT, EXPENDITURE AND INCOME

Output

The output measure of GDP is obtained by combining value added (value of production less cost of inputs) by all businesses: agriculture, mining, manufacturing and services. Output data are usually presented in index form (that is, with a base year such as 1985 equal to 100).

Sectors. In general countries have larger agricultural sectors in the early stages of economic development (for example, sub-Saharan Africa, see Figure 3.1). The manufacturing sector's share of output increases as the economy develops (Asia-Pacific) and services take

29

Figure 3.1

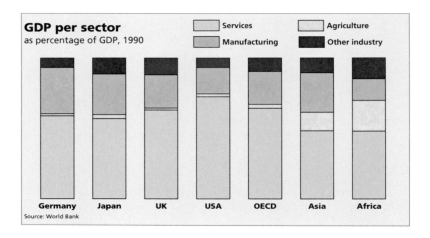

the largest share of output in mature economies (America).

Highly detailed data are often available. The production of tens or hundreds of goods and services industries may be recorded separately. For example, there will probably be an appropriate index in the GDP output breakdown to allow you to compare the performance of, say, a furniture manufacturing company with that of the industry as a whole. The industrialised countries generally publish more detailed (and more up-to-date) statistics than less developed countries.

Classifications. Economic information has to be categorised, but the correct classification is not always self-evident. For example, should the production of man-made fibres from petroleum be recorded under textiles (as they generally used to be) or chemicals (as they are now)?

Standards have been introduced to deal with these problems and provide consistency. Industrial production, retail trade, imports and exports are classified according to standard themes. Many countries now follow the United Nations' international standard industrial classification (ISIC), while European nations tend to use the similar EC *Nomenclature générale des activités dans les Communautés Européennes* (NACE). These are fairly detailed and they need revision from time to time.

For example, if the standard industrial classification (SIC) introduced in the UK in 1948 had not been revised several times, computer manufacturing would be classified under office equipment, which is part of non-electrical engineering.

When making sectoral comparisons between two or more countries, try to find out if the sectors are made up of the same industries, otherwise there may be inconsistencies in the comparison.

Expenditure

The expenditure measure of GDP is obtained by adding up all spending:

consumption (spending on items such as food and clothing)
+ investment (spending on houses, factories, and so on)
= total domestic expenditure
+ exports of goods and services (foreigners' spending)
= total final expenditure
− imports of goods and services (spending abroad)
= GDP

Government consumption. The level of government spending reflects the role of the state. Government consumption is generally 10–20% of GDP, although it is higher in countries such as Denmark and Sweden where the state provides many services. Changes in government spending tend to reflect political decisions rather than market forces.

Private consumption. This is also called personal consumption or consumer expenditure. It is generally the largest individual category of spending (but see exports, below). In the industrialised countries consumption is around 60% of GDP. The ratio is much higher in poor countries which invest less and consume more.

Investment. Investment is perhaps the key structural component of spending since it lays down the basis for future production. It covers spending on factories, machinery, equipment, dwellings and inventories of raw materials and other items. Investment averages about 20% of GDP in the industrialised countries, but is nearer 30% of GDP in the rapidly growing Asia-Pacific countries (see Figure 3.2).

Consumption or investment? There are some anomalies in the identification of consumption and investment. Government spending on roads, defence and education is generally scored as consumption rather than investment. Consumer spending on cars and other durable goods (items with a life of over one year) is considered to be consumption. Capital goods purchased by a financial institution and leased to an industrial company are also usually classified as consumption. Thus consumption tends to be overstated and investment under-recorded.

Figure 3.2

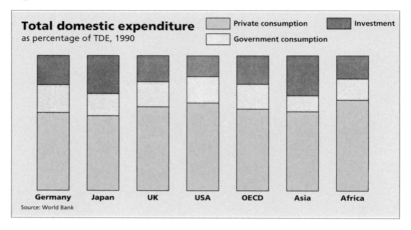

Total domestic expenditure as percentage of TDE, 1990

Private consumption   Investment   Government consumption

Germany   Japan   UK   USA   OECD   Asia   Africa
Source: World Bank

Total domestic expenditure (TDE). Consumption plus investment is known as total domestic expenditure. This is a useful concept because it measures domestic spending, some of which goes on imported goods and services. It under-records sales because it does not include those goods and services sold abroad (exports).

Total final expenditure/output (TFE/TFO). Consumption and investment plus exports of goods and services is known as total final expenditure. This takes account of the fact that some consumer and investment goods and services are purchased by foreigners.

Another way of looking at this is as total final output: the value of home-produced and imported goods and services available for consumption, investment or export.

TFE and TFO are identical in coverage. The difference is in the terminology, which depends on whether the emphasis is on output or spending. Since some expenditure goes on goods and services originating overseas, TFE/TFO has to be reduced by the amount of imports of goods and services to give total output.

Exports and imports. Exports generate foreign currency income, while imports are a leakage of domestic spending into another country's production. These external transactions can have an important effect on GDP.

Some countries have a low dependence on external trade. American imports and exports are each about 10% of GDP. Other countries, especially those on the Pacific rim, are heavily dependent on external flows. Hong Kong and Singapore, both trading

Figure 3.3

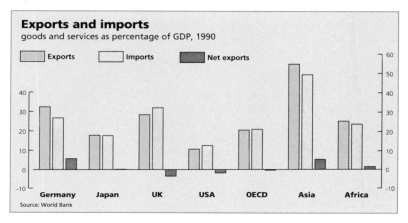

economies, have imports and exports, each of which are 100–200% of GDP (many imports are re-exported). These are open economies, while America is relatively closed (see Figure 3.3). Open economies have greater opportunity for export-led growth but are also more vulnerable to external shocks.

Income

The income measure of GDP is based on total incomes from production. It is essentially the total of:

- wages and salaries of employees;
- income from self-employment;
- trading profits of companies;
- trading surpluses of government corporations and enterprises; and
- income from rents.

These are known as factor incomes. GDP does not include transfer payments such as interest and dividends, pensions, or other social security benefits. The breakdown of incomes sheds additional light on economic behaviour because it is the counterpart to expenditure in what economists call the circular flow of money. It also provides a useful basis for forecasting inflation.

Accounting conventions. Incomes data are collected from figures which are based on common accounting conventions, rather than the principles of national accounting. One result is that reported company profits include any increase or decrease in the value of inventories. A value (as opposed to a volume) change does not represent any real economic activity, so this stock appreciation is deducted from total domestic income to arrive at GDP.

Discrepancies

In a perfect world, the output, expenditure and income measures would be identical. In practice there are discrepancies due to inevitable shortcomings in data collection, differences in the reported timing of transactions and the black economy. The discrepancy between any pair of measures is typically up to 1–2% of GDP. It can be much larger than this, as it was in many countries in the mid-1970s when data collection was complicated by sharp oil price increases and rapid inflation.

Since output, expenditure and income data are, by and large, collected independently, the safest approach is to take the average of the three as indicative of overall economic trends. Not many governments, however, publish such averages and it may not be practical to calculate them. Consequently it is usually necessary to focus on one.

The output measure is usually the most reliable indicator of short-term developments (that is, up to one year) as the survey data are fairly concrete. For longer periods the expenditure measure is probably better, mainly because the weights used to aggregate the output indicators are only updated at infrequent intervals and they become out of date. The income measure is usually the last available and least reliable.

PRICES

Market prices and factor cost

Many transactions are subject to taxes and subsidies. Sales tax or value-added tax (VAT) and subsidised housing are obvious examples. The expenditure measure of GDP records market prices, which includes these taxes and subsidies. The income and output measures are generally reported at factor cost (that is, they exclude taxes and subsidies). The relationship is simple:

GDP at market prices
− indirect taxes
+ subsidies   } factor cost adjustment
= GDP at factor cost

The factor cost adjustment. The factor cost adjustment (the net total of taxes and subsidies) enables the income, expenditure and output measures to be converted freely between factor cost and market prices. This allows consistent comparisons and highlights the effect of government intervention.

National conventions. Americans tend to measure economic activity at market prices right through to the net national product stage. They then adjust for taxes and subsidies to reach national income at factor cost. Thus a reference to American GDP probably means GDP at market prices. At the other end of the spectrum, the British publish many figures at both factor cost and market prices all the way through. Loose reference to British GDP usually means the expenditure measure at market prices. GDP on an income or output basis is probably at factor cost while the expenditure measures are usually at market prices, but the only way to be sure is to check the basis of the figures in question.

Current and constant prices

GDP figures are reported in current and constant prices.

- Output data are generally collected in both current and constant prices. The constant price figures for each industry are obtained by valuing current output in the prices applicable in a given base year; say, 1982 or 1985.
- Expenditure data are mostly collected in current prices. They are converted into constant prices by the same adjustment process used with output data, or – slightly differently – by deflating each component by an estimated price indicator. Once the current and constant price versions of the expenditure measure are available, they are used to calculate an overall deflator (that is, the price index) which is used with the income measure.
- Income data are collected in current prices and converted into constant prices using deflators derived from the expenditure measure.

The deflator. The GDP deflator calculated from expenditure data at factor cost is also known as the implicit price deflator. This is a handy measure of economy-wide inflation trends, but it is affected by changes in the composition of GDP (see page 208).

Adjusting for inflation is less reliable at times when prices are changing rapidly. Small errors in the measurements of current values and prices can combine to create large errors in the constant price series. Make it a rule to question the accuracy of price deflators. For example, 12% nominal GDP growth with inflation of 10%

35

results in approximately 2% real growth in GDP. If inflation is actually slightly higher, at 11%, real GDP growth is halved to a mere 1%.

PUTTING IT IN CONTEXT

Population

The notes on omissions (pages 27–28) suggest that output figures are a dubious guide to the quality of life. Nevertheless, total output per head (that is, GDP divided by the size of the population) is used as a broad indicator of living standards. A rise in real GDP that is greater than any increase in population is taken to indicate an improvement in economic well-being. However, if, for example, real GDP increases by 3% while population expands by 5%, the economy is "worse off" (that is, real GDP per head has declined).

Purchasing power

Output per head in current prices is a useful guide to levels of economic activity when making "snapshot" comparisons between countries. Since it is necessary, however, to convert the figures into a common currency, the underlying message can be distorted by exchange rate effects.

The best solution is to use output per head on a purchasing power parity (PPP) basis, which adjusts for national variations in the prices paid for goods and services. This is not easy to calculate accurately, but some intergovernmental agencies such as the OECD produce estimates. Their figures show, for example, that although Switzerland's GDP per head is 40% higher than that of America if converted into dollars at current exchange rates, after adjusting for variations in prices the spending power of the Swiss is more than 10% below that of Americans (see page 43).

Employment

Another way of measuring relative activity is with output per person employed. This is an important measure of productivity which is discussed extensively in Chapter 4.

RELIABILITY

Some problems of obtaining information by surveys and samples are outlined above. In addition, the rush to publish information often means that figures are revised several times as new information comes to hand, perhaps causing major changes in interpretation. For example, industrial production figures may be based initially on sales and output data and adjusted later to take account of changes in inventories not caught in the sales figures. Statisticians go to great lengths to account for these and other problems. The techniques employed are reasonably reliable, at least in the more developed nations. It is important to remember, however, that published figures for GDP, average earnings, prices, and so on are only estimates.

Moreover, the basis on which some figures are calculated by less scrupulous governments does not stand up to close examination. Consumer-price indices are particularly vulnerable. They may include only selected subsidised goods and services and omit those which increase in price too rapidly.

The good statistics guide

In 1991 *The Economist* asked a panel of statisticians in various countries to rank government statistical agencies in the ten largest industrialised countries according to the perceived reliability of their figures. Canada came out top, followed closely by Australia, Sweden and Holland (see Table 3.1). Britain and Italy were bottom of the list.

Table 3.1 **Number-crunchers ranked**

	Statisticians' ranking	Revisions[a] percentage points	Timeliness[b]
Canada	1	1.0	10
Australia	2	1.7	8
Sweden	3	2.4	5
Holland	4	1.6	9
France	5	1.3	6
Germany	6	3.0	1
USA	7	1.1	4
Japan	8	2.7	7
UK	9	1.7	1
Italy	10	1.7	1

[a] The change between the initial and final estimates of GDP for 1987–89.
[b] The average speed of publication of GDP, industrial production, consumer prices and trade figures, where 1 is fastest and 10 is slowest.

Source: The Economist, September 7th 1991

The Economist also looked at the size of revisions in each country. Canada did well again with the smallest revisions to its figures in the 1987–89 period. America and France similarly revised their figures relatively little, while Germany and Japan revised theirs substantially.

However, Canada was also among the slowest to produce economic indicators, taking until the third week of June 1991 to publish first quarter GDP data. Germany, Britain and Italy were the fastest to get their numbers out, which may give some excuse for the large revisions.

Perhaps the bottom line is that the reliability of economic indicators must always be questioned, and it is useful to try to develop a feel for their accuracy.

4

GROWTH: TRENDS AND CYCLES

"When your neighbour loses his job, it's a slowdown; when you lose your job, it's a recession; when an economist loses his job, it's a depression."
Anon

Chapter 3 focused on national income as a snapshot of economic activity. This chapter considers the interesting question of changes in economic activity over time. The introduction outlines the basic issues which affect growth. The GDP briefs explain how to interpret indicators of overall activity. The productivity brief shows how employment and investment lay down the basis for long-term growth. Finally the brief on cyclical indicators indicates the way that many economic series fluctuate around the trend.

Trends and cycles

Economic developments should be judged in the context of trends and cycles.

Trends. The trend is the long-term rate of economic expansion. The industrial economies have enjoyed a growth trend for decades or even centuries. Since the second world war the volume of goods and services that they produce has grown by 3–4% a year in general and a sparkling 7% a year in Japan. Figure 4.1 shows the 1947–90 trend for the American economy.

Cycles. The cycle reflects short-term fluctuations around the trend. There are always a few months or years when growth is above trend, followed by a period when the economy contracts or grows below trend (see Figure 4.1).

Sources of growth

Long-term growth. In the long term the growth in economic output depends on the number of people working and output per worker (productivity).

Clearly there are limits to changes in the size of the population

Figure 4.1

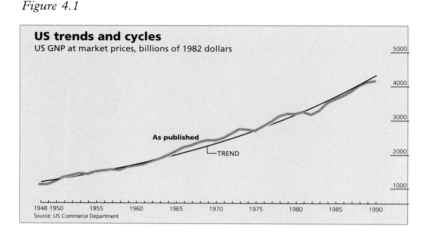

and the number of people in employment. On the other hand, only an extreme pessimist can see an end to long-term productivity improvements. Output per worker grows through technical progress and investment in new plant, machinery and equipment. Investment and productivity are therefore the basis for continued and sustained economic expansion.

The Productivity brief (page 49) quantifies the relationship between employment, investment and growth. It is important to distinguish between economic growth, which may reflect nothing more than an expanding population, and overall economic welfare which, if measured by the volume of goods and services produced per person, improves only if output grows faster than the population.

See GDP and GDP per head, pages 41–44.

Short-term cycles. The brief on Cyclical indicators (page 51) explains the way that economic growth fluctuates around the trend. The brief is important because it lays the basis for interpreting many economic indicators. For example, a downturn in housing starts or an increase in inventories may signal a recession perhaps 12 months hence.

The circular flow of incomes. Firms and households are the backbone of an economy. Firms employ people to make goods and provide services. This gives households their incomes. Household spending provides the rationale for the existence of firms. Thus the circular flow continues; in short, output = income = expenditure.

There are leakages from and injections to the circular flow.

Money is taken out of circulation when people buy imports, save or pay taxes. This means less spending, so firms sell fewer goods and services. Money is put into circulation when people run down their savings or borrow, when governments spend their taxes and when foreigners buy exports. These actions boost spending, so firms sell more goods and services.

All leakages and injections affect spending power and influence savings and investment decisions. These may be thought of as causing cyclical variations while productivity determines long-term growth. Life is never simple, of course, and productivity depends on investment, which in turn depends on many factors including the cycle itself.

Inflation and volumes

Higher demand can easily result in inflation. For example, if employers increase wages without raising output, and if the extra incomes are spent in full, prices will be pulled up (demand-pull inflation) but there will be no increase in real welfare.

The effects of inflation are wide and far-reaching. They are particularly relevant when analysing small parts of the economy in great detail, such as when projecting earnings and share prices for one company. For assessing the economy as a whole it is better to focus on the volume of output rather than its nominal money value, and to think in volume or inflation-adjusted constant price terms. These concepts are discussed in Chapter 2; Chapter 13 reviews inflation in detail.

NOMINAL GDP

Measures: Total economic activity in current prices.
Significance: Describes the total level of production. Use as a yardstick for measuring "economic achievement" or other indicators (such as the current-account balance as a percentage of GDP).
Presented as: Quarterly and annual totals.
Focus on: Totals. Use factor cost when reviewing output or incomes, market prices if looking at expenditure patterns.
Yardstick: The OECD total was $16,000 billion in 1990.
Released: Quarterly, 1–3 months in arrears; frequently revised.

Interpretation

Nominal GDP or GNP is used to measure total economic activity. The choice between the two depends largely on national conventions (see page 26). Where GDP is higher than GNP it indicates net investment income from abroad.

The annual total ranges from under $1 billion in some African countries to over $5,000 billion in America. For countries at similar stages of development, magnitude depends largely on population size. (See GDP per head and Real GDP, pages 43 and 44.)

Table 4.1   **Nominal GDP, 1990**
(values in billions)

	% of total	$	$PPP[a]	GDP national currency[b]	GNP national currency[b]	GNP as % of GDP
Australia	1.8	295	272	380	362	95.4
Belgium	1.2	192	163	6429	6352	98.8
Canada	3.5	570	509	665	641	9
France	7.3	1191	983	6484	6467	99.7
Germany	9.2	1488	1157	2405	2426	100.9
Holland	1.7	279	236	508	509	100.1
Italy	6.7	1091	924	1306833	1290975	98.8
Japan	18.1	2943	2178	426107	429173	100.7
Spain	3.0	491	459	50074	49627	99.1
Sweden	1.4	228	144	1350	1313	97.2
Switzerland	1.4	225	143	312	326	104.4
UK	6.0	975	902	549	548	99.7
USA	33.2	5392	5392	5392	5441	100.9
EC	37.1	6015	5112			
OECD	100.0	16226	14268			

[a] Purchasing power parity; where output is adjusted for variations in spending power.
[b] National currencies are identified in Table 11.1.

Source: OECD

Figure 4.2

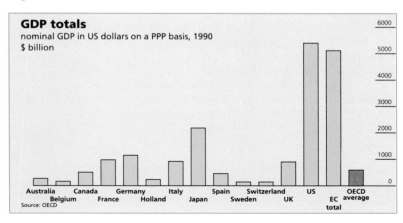

GDP totals
nominal GDP in US dollars on a PPP basis, 1990
$ billion

Australia   Canada   Germany   Italy   Spain   Switzerland   US   OECD average
Belgium   France   Holland   Japan   Sweden   UK   EC total
Source: OECD

Figure 4.3

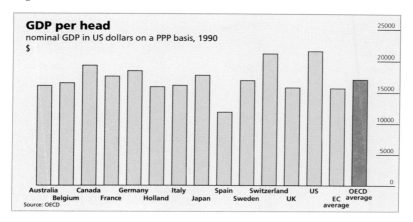

GDP per head — nominal GDP in US dollars on a PPP basis, 1990. Source: OECD

GDP PER HEAD

Measures:	Output per person; GDP or GDP divided by population size.
Significance:	Used as an indicator of overall economic welfare.
Presented as:	Quarterly and annual totals.
Focus on:	Nominal totals; changes in real terms.
Yardstick:	The OECD average was $19,000 per head in 1990.
Released:	Annually, sometimes quarterly; well in arrears; frequently revised.

What to look for

Output per head is a good guide to living standards. It implicitly allows for qualitative factors such as literacy or health although these are not covered directly.

In the early 1990s annual output per head was less than $100 in some African states, while the world median was somewhere around $1,000. The output of the rich industrial countries was at least ten times greater. After adjusting for variations in purchasing power, North America had the highest figure, at around $20,000. Switzerland, Japan and the Nordic countries are close behind.

If real GDP per head increases it indicates an improvement in overall economic well-being.

43

Table 4.2   **GDP per head, 1990**

	$	$PPP[a]	National currency[b]	Real GDP annual % change 1960–89	1990
				Nominal GDP	Real GDP
Australia	17266	15919	22216	2.3	−0.0
Belgium	19264	16354	645063	3.1	3.5
Canada	21412	19121	24990	3.0	−1.0
France	21110	17423	114926	3.0	2.1
Germany	23532	18298	38027	2.7	2.8
Holland	18666	15789	34007	2.3	3.2
Italy	18926	16029	22669575	3.5	1.7
Japan	23822	17630	3449142	5.4	5.3
Spain	12603	11782	1285302	3.7	3.4
Sweden	26639	16824	157745	2.5	−0.1
Switzerland	33108	21042	45962	1.9	1.1
UK	16983	15711	9566	2.2	0.5
USA	21448	21448	21449	2.1	−0.1
EC	18363	15607	na	2.9	2.2
OECD	19333	17000	na	2.8	1.3

[a] Purchasing power parity; output per head adjusted for variations in spending power.
[b] National currencies are identified in Table 11.1.

Source: OECD

REAL GDP

Measures: Total economic activity in constant prices.
Significance: Most useful for tracking developments over time.
Presented as: Quarterly and annual totals.
Focus on: Percentage changes, annual or over four quarters.
Yardstick: The OECD average was 2.7% a year growth during the 1980s.
Released: Quarterly, 1–3 months in arrears; frequently revised.

What to look for

Real (constant price) GDP or GDP figures reveal changes in economic output after adjusting for inflation. These should be put in the context of the cycle (see Cyclical indicators, page 51). Strong economic growth following a recession may simply indicate that slack capacity is being put back into use (see Capacity use and Unemployment, pages 107 and 63).

Strong growth when the economy is already buoyant may indicate the installation of new capacity which will add still more to future output (see Investment, Chapter 8). However, excess growth at the top of the cycle may bubble over into inflation and/or imports (see Chapter 13).

Developing countries have the capacity for faster GDP growth than more mature industrial economies. Real growth of around 3% per annum is good for America and Europe. A rate of at least double that (that is, over 6 per cent per annum) is expected of the newly industrialising countries on the Pacific rim.

The inflation/output trade-off

The change in real GDP plus the change in the deflator (see page 35) approximately equals the change in nominal GDP. For example, if real output rises by 3% and inflation is 5%, nominal output has risen by about 8%. Some economists argue that aggregate demand determines nominal GDP and that there is a trade-off between real output and inflation: each can rise by any amount so long as the total equals the change in nominal output. Higher inflation therefore means lower growth in output.

World cycles

For the industrialised world, 1960, 1968, 1973 and 1979 were peak years for economic activity. There was another peak around the start of the 1990s, although a longer period of hindsight is needed before this can be dated precisely (see Cyclical indicators, page 51). Table 4.3 shows economic growth rates within each cycle, which provide useful yardsticks for judging future growth rates.

Industrial economies. The 1960s were a period of rapid expansion, due at least in part to technological advances and freedom from external shocks. The 1973 and 1979 oil price rises caused temporary setbacks. Japan was perhaps more badly hit by the first; Europe and America suffered more from the second. Growth was rapid again in the mid-late 1980s. The mid-decade fall in oil prices and policy responses to it may have helped extend the cycle, but many countries failed to get total output back up to trend.

Developing countries. The oil producers enjoyed rapid growth rates in the 1970s and suffered the greatest setbacks in the 1980s. Broadly similar patterns were recorded by many Latin American and African countries, with the slowdown in the 1980s reflecting the debt crisis, a lack of inward investment, and foreign-exchange shortages. East European countries also had feeble growth in the 1980s, reflecting the shortcomings of their planned economies.

45

Table 4.3   **Four world cycles**
Annual % change in real GDP

	Four cycles				Two cycles disaggregated			
					down	up	down	up
	1960–68	68–73	73–79	79–90	1973–75	75–79	79–83	83–90
Australia	5.0	5.3	2.6	3.1	1.8	3.0	1.5	4.0
Belgium	4.6	5.6	2.3	2.2	1.3	2.8	1.3	2.7
Canada	5.5	5.4	4.3	2.8	3.5	4.7	1.1	3.7
France	5.4	5.5	2.8	2.1	1.4	3.5	1.5	2.6
Germany	4.0	4.9	2.3	2.0	−0.6	3.9	0.6	2.9
Holland	5.0	4.7	2.6	1.7	1.9	3.0	0.1	2.7
Italy	5.7	4.6	3.7	2.4	1.3	4.9	1.7	2.9
Japan	10.1	8.8	3.6	4.1	1.0	4.9	3.3	4.6
Spain	7.5	6.6	2.2	2.8	2.9	1.9	1.0	3.8
Sweden	4.4	3.8	1.8	1.9	3.0	1.2	1.1	2.4
Switzerland	4.4	4.6	−0.2	2.3	−2.8	1.1	1.5	2.8
UK	3.0	3.3	1.5	2.1	−1.1	2.9	0.5	3.1
USA	4.5	3.0	2.6	2.6	−0.9	4.3	0.7	3.7
EC	4.3	4.7	2.4	2.2	0.0	3.6	0.9	2.9
OECD	5.2	4.2	2.8	2.7	−0.4	4.4	1.3	3.6

Source: OECD

GDP: OUTPUT

Measures: GDP according to sector (agriculture, mining, manufacturing and service industries).
Significance: Provides analysis of total output at a high level of detail.
Presented as: Quarterly and annual totals.
Focus on: Real growth rates.
Yardstick: Overall real growth in the GDP total.
Released: Quarterly, 1–3 months in arrears; frequently revised.

What to look for

Compare the percentage change in each sector with the overall percentage change in GDP. A sector which is growing faster than the average is making a very positive contribution to growth. A sector which is growing less rapidly than the average is clawing it down.

A change in a dominant sector has a larger effect on total activity than a change in a smaller sector. For example, in the industrial economies a 1% rise in services boosts GDP by more than a similar increase in agriculture. Indeed, the mature industrialised countries are undergoing a shift from manufacturing to services. In the big seven economies annual growth in services was 3.2% over the past two cycles (1973–89) compared with 2.6% in manufacturing.

Figure 4.4

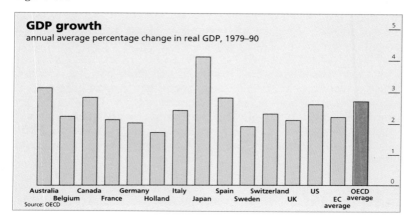

In general developing countries depend more on agriculture or, if they are at a later stage of development, manufacturing.

Chapter 9 reviews individual indicators of output.

Table 4.4 **Dominant sectors**
Output as % of GDP

		General trend
Agriculture		
Cambodia	90	undeveloped
Laos	75	↓
Manufacturing		
Macau	40	developing
Puerto Rico	40	↓
Services		
Bahamas	80	developed
USA	70	

Source: World Bank

GDP: EXPENDITURE

Measures: GDP according to category of spending (consumption, investment and net exports).
Significance: Provides detailed analysis of total spending.
Presented as: Quarterly and annual totals.
Focus on: Real growth rates.
Yardstick: Overall real growth in the GDP total.
Released: Quarterly, 1–3 months in arrears; frequently revised.

What to look for

As with the GDP output breakdown, compare the percentage change in each category of spending with the overall percentage growth in GDP in the same period.

Personal consumption. Growth in this category often leads a general recovery from recession, encouraging manufacturers to invest more. However, if consumption grows faster than the productive capacity of an economy, imports are sucked in and inflation rises. Personal consumption typically accounts for 60% of GDP, so a change in consumption has a big effect on total output.

Government spending. This reflects, to some extent, politics rather than market forces. Its share in GDP is higher in countries where the state provides many services. A short-term increase in government spending can provide a stabilising boost to the economy, but in general it diverts resources from productive growth.

Investment. This is a key component, contributing to current growth and laying down the foundation for future expansion. Look for spending on machinery (which produces more output) rather than, say, dwellings.

Changes in stocks. These can be erratic. They decline when demand is growing more rapidly than production (a good sign at the beginning of a recovery, potentially inflationary at the end) or when manufacturers and distributors are squeezed and are trying to cut the cost of holding stocks. Inventories tend to rise when demand slows.

Exports and imports. Exports contribute to overall GDP growth; higher imports reduce the increase in output relative to the growth in demand. A sudden increase in import penetration (imports divided by GDP) suggests that consumer demand is growing faster than the domestic economy can cope with (overheating). A longer-term increase in imports relative to exports implies a decline in the competitiveness of an industrialised economy. Imports that are substantially larger than exports may point to exchange-rate problems.

PRODUCTIVITY

Measures: Output for one unit of labour or capital.
Significance: Indicator of efficiency and potential total economic output.
Presented as: Index numbers.
Focus on: Trend, especially relative to other countries.
Yardstick: OECD average growth in real output per worker was 1.7% a year during the 1980s.
Released: Sometimes monthly, often two months in arrears; frequently revised.

Overview

Productivity measures the amount of output that is produced with given amounts of factor inputs (mainly land, labour and capital). Land is basically fixed and capital is very difficult to measure, so attention tends to focus on labour productivity. This can be defined in various ways. The most common are as follows.

- Output per worker = total output divided by total employment.
- Output per man hour = total output divided by hours worked.

Labour productivity reflects capital investment and offers a guide to capital productivity. A company using high-tech machinery will probably produce more per person than a company using nine-teenth century steam technology (such as in eastern Europe). Other factors which affect labour productivity include social attitudes, work ethics, unionisation and, perhaps most important, training. These are not measured directly by economic statistics.

The arithmetic of growth

Economic growth reflects growth of the labour force plus growth of labour productivity.

Labour productivity in turn depends on new investment (which raises the capital:labour ratio, which is known as factor substitution in economic jargon) and technological progress (which increases output for a given capital:labour ratio).

Table 4.5 shows trends in the major industrial economies. Data are presented in terms of four economic cycles (see Cyclical indicators, page 51).

Interpretation

Productivity figures can be calculated in money terms, but they are generally produced as index numbers. As a result, analysts

49

Table 4.5   **Sources of economic growth in industrial economies**
Annual % change

	Golden age 1960–73	Inflation & slump 1973–79	Consolidation 1979–89	1990[a]
Technological progress	2.8	0.6	0.8	1.2
Factor substitution[b]	1.3	0.9	1.0	0.9
Total labour productivity	4.1	1.5	1.7	2.1
Labour input[c]	1.1	1.4	1.0	0.8
Total output	5.2	2.9	2.7	2.9

[a] World Bank "baseline" forecasts.
[b] Growth in the capital:labour ratio × the share of profits in national income.
[c] Growth in employment corrected for (falling) hours worked per week.

Source: World Bank

often look at changes over time and disregard the important question of the base from which the index numbers are calculated. If this was a period of high or low productivity, changes will be distorted.

Nevertheless, trends are important. If output per person increases by 5%, an identical increase in wage rates may leave profitability unchanged. Indeed, since total labour costs (including, for example, the cost of providing recreational facilities for workers) may increase less rapidly than wages, profitability may actually improve. (See Wages and Unit labour costs, pages 198 and 202.)

Cycles. Productivity is highly cyclical since employment and capital are less flexible than demand and output. When production falls after a peak in economic activity, employment declines less rapidly and output per head plummets.

When demand for goods and services increases after a recession, slack capacity is called into use and productivity rises rapidly.

Comparisons

When comparing absolute levels of productivity (rather than trends) remember that productivity also depends on technology and costs. Companies in Asia have a lower dollar value of output per person, but can still be more profitable than European or American companies because labour costs are cheaper in Asia.

Exchange-rate changes are also important for international comparisons of competitiveness (see page 154).

50

Table 4.6   **Growth of productivity**
Annual % change in real GDP per worker

	Four cycles			Two cycles disaggregated			
	1960–68	68–73	73–79	79–90	down 1973–75	up 75–79	down 79–83	up 83–90
Australia	2.4	2.6	1.8	0.8	0.9	2.2	0.7	0.8
Belgium	4.0	4.9	2.3	2.2	1.3	2.8	2.4	1.9
Canada	2.3	2.4	1.4	1.0	0.5	1.8	0.4	1.4
France	4.9	4.3	2.5	2.1	1.5	3.0	1.7	2.3
Germany	4.1	4.3	2.8	1.4	1.5	3.5	0.5	1.9
Holland	3.8	4.1	2.3	1.4	2.2	2.4	1.4	1.4
Italy	6.2	4.9	2.8	2.0	0.0	4.1	1.3	2.4
Japan	8.5	7.7	2.9	3.0	1.4	3.6	2.1	3.4
Spain	6.9	5.7	3.2	2.5	3.3	3.2	3.2	2.1
Sweden	4.0	3.0	0.5	1.1	0.6	0.5	0.8	1.4
Switzerland	2.9	3.1	0.7	1.4	−0.4	1.2	0.2	2.2
UK	2.7	3.1	1.3	1.6	−0.9	2.5	2.2	1.2
USA	2.6	0.7	0.0	0.9	−1.3	0.7	0.2	1.2
EC	4.1	4.2	2.3	1.7	0.2	3.3	1.4	1.8
OECD	4.1	2.9	1.6	1.7	−0.6	2.8	1.0	2.2

Source: OECD

CYCLICAL OR LEADING INDICATORS

Measures: The economic cycle.
Significance: Useful tool for short-term predictions of economic activity.
Presented as: Index numbers.
Focus on: Trends.
Yardstick: Look for turning points.
Released: Monthly, at least one month in arrears; frequently revised.

Overview

In developed economies at least, GDP progresses erratically around its long-term growth trend. There are periods when growth spurts ahead, followed by periods of recession. This variation is known as the economic, business or trade cycle. It repeats every five years or so, although no two cycles are ever of the same magnitude or duration.

The cycle has four phases: expansion, peak, recession and trough.

Expansion. When demand first increases, for whatever reason, it gathers momentum automatically. The first sign is often a rundown in inventories. Output then rises faster than demand while

51

these are rebuilt (see Inventories, page 96). Companies take on unemployed workers, who spend their new income on postponed purchases of consumer goods. This creates more demand and companies employ more people, and so the process continues (the multiplier). Before long producers come up against capacity constraints. If they are confident that demand will remain buoyant (expectations), they invest more in new plant and machinery, which generates even more demand (the accelerator).

Peak. The upward momentum cannot continue indefinitely. Eventually output hits a ceiling due to bottlenecks and supply constraints. Demand for investment funds may push up interest rates to the point where new investment is not profitable, or at full employment there may be no more workers to take on. Consumer demand may be steady, but the fall in investment demand pulls back the level of total output.

Recession. With investment demand falling, producers of capital goods start to cut back on labour. Higher unemployment reduces consumer demand. The inventories, multiplier, expectations and accelerator principles work in reverse and the economic contraction gathers momentum.

Trough. Output will not fall indefinitely. It will stop at some minimum level (a trough or depression) because employees retain jobs and spending power where they work in government or in industries supplying food, basic essentials and perhaps export goods. Unemployment and welfare payments, past saving and new borrowing enable other consumers to buy essentials.

Slack demand for investment funds may pull back interest rates making new or replacement investment attractive, at least for the industries providing basic essentials. And with consumer demand steady, investment demand begins to lift the economy again.

In America a recession is technically defined as two consecutive quarters of falling GDP. The snag with this is that if GDP plunges steeply in the first and third quarters of a year, but rises slightly in the second and fourth quarters, then officially an economy has escaped a recession, even though output may end the year sharply lower. Some economists prefer to define a recession as a year-on-year fall in output. Others talk about a "growth recession" when a country's GDP growth rate falls below its long-term productive potential. In Japan, for example, annual growth of less than 3% is commonly called a recession.

Table 4.7 shows dates for the most recent peaks and troughs in *The Economist 13*.

Table 4.7 **Peaks and troughs in GDP**
Month/year

	Peak	Trough	Peak	Trough	Peak[a]
Australia	–	2/83	3/85	3/88	2/89
Belgium	1/80	–	–	1/87	–
Canada	1/79	4/82	–	–	1/89
France	3/79	–	–	1/85	–
Germany	1/80	4/82	–	–	–
Holland	4/79	1/83	–	–	–
Italy	1/80	2/83	–	–	–
Japan	1/80	4/83	2/85	2/87	–
Spain	1/80	2/85	–	–	–
Sweden	1/80	1/83	–	–	–
Switzerland	3/81	4/82	–	–	–
UK	2/79	3/82	–	–	4/88
USA	4/78	4/82	–	–	1/89
EC	1/80	2/84	–	–	–
OECD	1/80	4/82	–	–	–

Note: These peaks and troughs identified by the OECD may differ from those identified by national authorities.

[a] Provisional.

Source: OECD

Causes

There is no general consensus about what causes cycles or even about what is a cause and what is an effect. Major influences include fixed investment and inventory cycles, external shocks and well-meaning or perhaps self-interested government policies. It is not unknown for the government of the day to engineer an economic boom just before an election, thus setting the cycle in motion. Expansionary policies aimed at reducing unemployment followed by contractionary policies to limit the inflationary consequences can cause severe cyclical swings. Moreover, measures to cool a boom may be imposed when automatic contractionary forces are already in motion, thus hastening the downhill slide.

Cyclical patterns in economic indicators

Cyclical patterns can be detected in many economic series. Peaks and troughs do not fall in step. This means that indicators which turn in advance of GDP can be used to predict economic developments. The following timings indicate roughly what might be expected in a standard cycle in an industrial economy.

(Some economists argue that interest rates are a lagging indicator. They are included here as a leading indicator since most people are familiar with the idea of, say, lowering interest rates to boost a flagging economy.)

Leading indicators. Interest rates pass their low point and begin to rise about 18 months ahead of a peak in output.

Business confidence, share prices, housing starts and companies' financial surpluses peak 8–16 months ahead of output. Consumer credit, car sales and manufacturing orders peak about six months ahead. Retail sales peak 2–3 months in advance.

Coincident indicators. GDP establishes the reference point for the overall cycle, while other indicators which peak within a month or two of GDP are used to confirm that the economy is turning.

Lagging indicators. Manufacturing capacity utilisation peaks about a month after total output. Job vacancies peak about three months later, growth in average earnings after four months and growth in unit labour costs after five months. Productivity and unemployment stop falling and turn upwards six months after the peak in overall activity, and inflation peaks at about that time also. Investment, order backlogs and stocks peak around 12 months after output.

The cyclical indicators

Several countries and OECD statisticians have combined groups of economic indicators into composite cyclical indicators. Generally trends are removed, erratic fluctuations are smoothed, and the series are combined into weighted averages in index form.

The components of the indices vary, reflecting changes in economic habits and analysts' understanding of the economy. For example, in the early 1990s America downgraded the role of share prices after it was found that an increase in stockmarket values was taken as an indicator of an upturn, which prompted share buying and pushed up the leading indicator still further.

Interpretation. Use composite indicators as a guide to the cycle. Leading indicators turn 6–12 months ahead of GDP; coincident indicators turn with it; lagging indicators turn perhaps six months later.

Watch mainly for changes in direction in leading indicators and use coincident indicators to confirm the change. Most composite indicators are used only to identify turning points. However,

American indicators are scaled so that percentage changes are broadly suggestive of the magnitude of fluctuations in the overall level of economic activity.

Composite indicators are frequently published when only a few components are available and are revised in subsequent months as more information comes to hand and as component indicators are themselves revised. The composites should be interpreted with care and supplemented by examination of individual economic series.

5

POPULATION, EMPLOYMENT AND UNEMPLOYMENT

"Work is the refuge of people who have nothing better to do."
Oscar Wilde

This chapter contains a series of population and employment briefs. Among other things, they highlight the following points.

Trends. The first things to check when assessing longer-term economic trends are employment, productivity and investment. The brief on Productivity (page 49) shows their relationship to growth.

The size and age structure of the population provides an indicator of long-term pressures on the economy. GDP must grow at least as fast as the population if output per head is not to decline, while an increasing number of people of working age may signal enhanced productive potential, or more unemployment.

Cycles. Unemployment is an excellent indicator of the state of the economic cycle. High unemployment (compared with the average over the past few years) suggests a recessionary gap. Low unemployment at the top of the cycle is broadly indicative of inflationary pressures. Note, however, that unemployment lags the cycle by perhaps six months (see Cyclical indicators, page 51).

Services. The services sector accounts for 60–70% of output in the major industrialised countries, but it is relatively neglected among the commonly followed indicators of output. Employment provides a useful guide to activity in the sector.

Incomes. Employment data provide guides to personal incomes, wages and unit labour costs (see pages 80, 198 and 202). These are the basis for measuring GDP on an incomes basis and they help when assessing inflationary pressures.

POPULATION

Measures:	Total number of people in a country.
Significance:	Yardstick for minimum GDP growth.
Presented as:	Total number.
Focus on:	Age structure and changes.
Yardstick:	The OECD population grew by 0.7% a year in the 1980s. Average growth of 0.4% a year is forecast in 1990–2010.
Released:	Annually.

Overview

Real GDP must grow as least as fast as the population if living standards are not to fall. This may not be too hard in the industrial countries, where populations are expected to grow by less than 0.5% a year in 1990–2010. It will be more difficult in sub-Saharan Africa, where populations will increase by around 3% a year over the same period. Developing countries elsewhere are likely to expand a little less rapidly, except for some Arab states and, notably, China. The population of China is projected to surge by a staggering 11% a year in 1990–2010.

Migration and the age structure have important effects on output (see Labour or workforce, page 58).

Table 5.1 **Population**

	Total mid-1970 m	Total mid-1990 m	Growth 1990–2010 %[a]	Area '000km²
Australia	12.5	17.1	1.0	7687
Belgium	9.7	10.0	0.1	31
Canada	21.3	26.6	0.7	9976
France	50.8	56.4	0.3	552
Germany, West	60.7	63.1	−0.2	249
Germany, East	17.0	16.5	0.0	108
Holland	13.0	14.9	0.2	37
Italy	53.7	57.7	0.0	301
Japan	103.3	123.5	0.3	378
Spain	33.8	39.0	0.3	505
Sweden	8.0	8.6	0.0	450
Switzerland	6.2	6.7	−0.1	41
UK	55.4	57.4	−0.2	245
USA	205.0	250.0	0.6	9373
OECD	714.1	839.7	0.4	133609

[a] Predicted annual % change.

Sources: OECD; World Bank

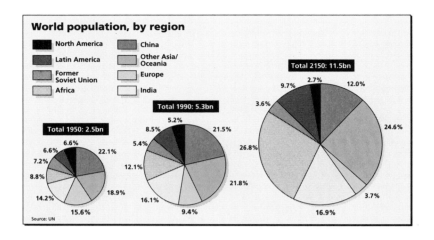

POPULATION GROWTH

The number of people in the world more than doubled between 1950 and 1990, up from 2.5 billion to 5.3 billion. The total will continue to rise but at a slower rate, reckons the United Nations, which forecasts a population of 11.5 billion in 2150. Since 1950 Europeans have become relatively scarce: more than 15% of people were European in 1950, but only 9.4% of them were in 1990. If the UN's forecast is accurate, Europeans will be rarer still in 2150 – accounting for just 3.7% of the total. The proportion of North Americans is forecast to fall, too, from 5.2% in 1990 to 2.7% in 2150. Africa's population is growing fastest, up from 8.8% of the total in 1950 to 12.1% in 1990. By 2150, says the UN, one person in four will be African.

The Economist, April 11th 1992

LABOUR OR WORKFORCE

Measures: Employees plus self-employed plus the unemployed.
Significance: Indicator of maximum potential output.
Presented as: Total number.
Focus on: Structure and changes.
Yardstick: The OECD labour force grew by 1.3% a year during the 1980s.
Released: Monthly, at least one month in arrears; see Employment, page 61.

Definitions

The labour force or workforce is the number of people employed and self-employed plus those unemployed but ready and able to work. The grand total is sometimes known as the economically active population. The components of the labour force are notoriously difficult to measure (see also Employment and Unemployment, pages 61 and 63).

The labour force is defined variously to include, for example, people whose age in years is over 14 (Italy), 15 (Canada), 16 (America), or in the range 16–64 (Sweden) or 16–74 (Norway).

There is a tendency to focus on the civilian labour force (that is, excluding the armed forces). Spain includes professional military personnel but excludes conscripts from its regular figures.

Changes in the labour force

The things to watch for are the three factors which affect the size of the labour force: population, migration and the proportion participating in economic activity.

Population. Birth rates in most industrial countries fell to replacement levels or lower in the 1980s. Meanwhile earlier population growth boosted to record levels the number of 15–24 year-olds entering the labour force (exceptions include Japan and Switzerland). This implies an older workforce and higher old-age dependency rates (the number of retired people as a percentage of the population of working age) in the future. Output per employee must grow for GDP per head to stand still. By 2010 15–20% of the population in industrial economies will be over 65 years of age.

Developing countries have young populations with up to 50% under 15 years. This suggests an expanding working-age population with potential problems for housing and job creation.

Migration. In the industrial countries inflows of foreign workers increased in the late 1980s and a substantial number of illegal immigrants were granted amnesty in America, France, Italy and Spain. Foreign-born persons account for over 5% of the labour force in America, Germany and France; around 20% in Switzerland and Canada; and over 25% in Australia.

Inward migration may be a bonus for some economies. For example, the unification of east and west Germany boosted that country's productive potential. However, large numbers of refugees seeking asylum can have significant adverse effects on income per head.

Wealthier developing countries, especially oil producers, have large proportions of foreigners in their labour forces. Workers frequently make a substantial contribution to the balance of payments in their home countries by remitting savings from their salaries.

Table 5.2 **Labour force**
(including armed forces)

	Size m 1990	Annual % change					
		Total				1990	Female 1979-89
		1960-68	1968-73	1973-79	1979-89		
Australia	8.5	2.7	2.7	1.5	2.4	2.7	3.9
Belgium	4.2	0.5	0.5	0.9	0.2	0.3	1.4
Canada	13.7	2.6	3.1	3.2	1.9	1.3	3.1
France	24.4	0.6	1.1	0.9	0.5	0.7	1.3
Germany	30.0	−0.1	0.7	−0.2	0.4	2.0	1.2
Holland	5.3	1.2	0.6	1.1	2.4	1.1	5.1
Italy	23.8	−0.6	−0.2	1.1	0.9	0.3	2.0
Japan	63.8	1.4	0.9	0.8	1.1	1.8	1.6
Spain	15.0	0.7	0.9	0.1	1.2	1.4	3.0
Sweden	4.6	0.5	0.8	1.2	0.6	1.1	1.3
Switzerland	3.6	1.4	1.5	−0.9	1.2	1.2	1.7
UK	28.5	0.4	0.2	0.6	0.7	0.0	1.6
USA	124.9	1.6	2.4	2.6	1.7	0.8	2.4
EC	144.2	0.2	0.5	0.6	0.9	0.8	1.9
OECD	392.3	0.9	1.3	1.3	1.3	1.1	2.1

Source: OECD

Figure 5.1

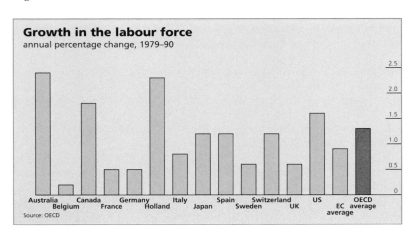

Growth in the labour force
annual percentage change, 1979–90

Source: OECD

Participation. Participation rates (the labour force as a percentage of the total population) generally increased in the 1980s and early 1990s with earlier retirement for men, especially in France, Finland and Holland, generally offset by more married women entering the labour force, especially in America, Australia, Britain, New Zealand and Scandinavia. Note the rapid growth in the female labour force shown in Table 5.2.

Women account for a smaller proportion of the workforce in Muslim countries (20%) and a greater proportion in Africa (up to 50%) where they traditionally work on the land.

EMPLOYMENT OR PAYROLLS AND HOURS WORKED

Measures:	Total employment = employees in employment plus the self-employed.
Significance:	Indicator of current output potential.
Presented as:	Totals.
Focus on:	Structure and changes.
Yardstick:	OECD employment grew by 1.2% a year during the 1980s.
Released:	Monthly, at least one month in arrears.

Data collection

Measuring employment is tricky. The main sources of data are censuses and surveys of population and employment. Household surveys are generally the most reliable since surveys of employers tend to double count people with more than one job.

Most countries conduct household surveys; some monthly (Australia, Japan, North America), some quarterly (Italy, New Zealand), some annually (Belgium, Greece) and some less frequently still (Turkey). Figures for months between main surveys are based on employment surveys or are estimates or interpolation.

Apart from the definitional problems mentioned in the previous brief, other distortions and international inconsistencies arise due to factors such as the method of counting home workers and domestic servants, part-time staff, people with more than one job, and those temporarily ill or laid off. Full employment is usually defined as the workforce less the natural rate of unemployment. (See also Unemployment, page 63.)

Basic analysis

The level of production depends on the number of people employed, hours worked, education, training and the quality of capital equipment. (See also Productivity, page 49.)

In turn, hours worked consists of core hours and overtime. There is a tendency for core hours to decline as economies mature and workers demand more leisure.

Interpretation

Employment and unemployment are highly cyclical. When demand increases, companies first tend to increase overtime. They take on more employees only when higher demand is perceived to be strong and durable. When demand turns down, hours are cut before jobs.

Watch hours worked and overtime for early signals, and employment for confirmation. Survey evidence (see Business conditions, page 103) indicating plans to take on or lay off workers may also provide early warning of changes in employment.

Try to identify to what extent an increase in payrolls represents second jobs. These limit employers' ability to increase output. A high number of second jobs with low unemployment suggest that any increase in consumer demand may be inflationary.

Sectoral trends. Where employment figures are available by sector, they provide a rough and ready guide to output trends in various parts of the economy. Employment in services is an imperfect but useful indicator for that sector since output data for service industries are hard to find.

Table 5.3 **Total employment**

	Total m	Annual % change				
	1990	1960–68	1968–73	1973–79	1979–89	1990
Australia	7.9	2.7	2.6	0.8	2.4	1.8
Belgium	3.8	0.6	0.6	0.0	0.0	0.9
Canada	12.6	2.8	2.8	2.9	1.8	0.7
France	22.2	0.4	1.1	0.3	0.1	1.2
Germany	28.5	−0.1	0.7	−0.5	0.5	2.6
Holland	5.0	1.1	0.5	0.5	0.1	2.1
Italy	21.1	−0.6	−0.3	0.8	0.4	1.4
Japan	62.5	1.5	0.9	0.7	1.0	2.0
Spain	12.6	0.7	1.0	−0.9	0.2	2.6
Sweden	4.5	0.5	0.7	1.3	0.7	0.9
Switzerland	3.6	1.4	1.5	−0.9	0.7	1.3
UK	26.8	0.3	0.2	0.2	0.5	0.3
USA	117.9	1.8	2.1	2.5	1.7	0.5
EC	132.1	0.1	0.5	0.1	0.5	1.5
OECD	367.6	1.0	1.2	1.0	1.2	1.2

Source: OECD

Figure 5.2

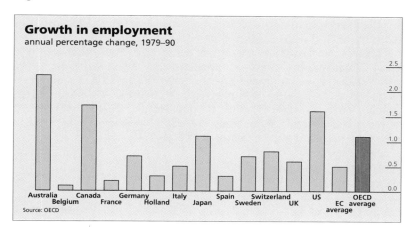

Growth in employment
annual percentage change, 1979–90

Source: OECD

UNEMPLOYMENT AND VACANCIES

Measures: Total = people out of work but ready and able to work.
Rate = unemployment as a percentage of the labour force.
Significance: Indicator of spare labour capacity (and wasted resources).
Presented as: Total number, percentage.
Focus on: Structure and changes.
Yardstick: The OECD standardised average was 7.3% in the 1980s.
Released: Monthly, at least one month in arrears.

Total unemployment. Based on people registered as unemployed (Austria, Switzerland) or claiming benefit (Belgium, Britain) or on survey evidence (many other countries). Surveys tend to make better indicators because they catch people who would take employment if work was available but who are not registered as unemployed.

Distortions and international inconsistencies arise due to factors such as students claiming benefits during vacations, the treatment of people temporarily laid off, discouraged workers who do not declare themselves available for work, and people who have part-time jobs but who are looking for full-time employment.

The unemployment rate. Usually defined as unemployment as a percentage of the labour force (the employed plus the unemployed). National variations are rife: Germany excludes the self-employed from the labour force; Belgium produces two unemployment rates expressing unemployment as a percentage of both the total and the insured labour force; Switzerland bases its

63

labour force on the 1980 census of population.

By changing the definition, which governments are inclined to do, the unemployment rate can be moved up or, more usually, down by several percentage points.

The International Labour Organisation (ILO) and other international organisations produce standardised unemployment rates which differ from national figures but which provide a consistent basis for cross-country comparisons. Note how the British and Dutch national figures are 1 percentage point below the "standardised rates", while Italy manages to overstate its unemployment rate by a similar amount (Table 5.4).

Table 5.4 **Unemployment**
(Standardised definition, as % of labour force)

		Unemployment rate					Long-term unemployed[a]	
	1964–67	1968–73	1974–79	1980–89	1990	1990[b]	1981–89	1989
Australia	1.6	2.0	5.0	7.5	6.9	6.9	26.8	23.0
Belgium	2.0	2.5	6.3	10.8	7.3	8.8	70.9	76.3
Canada	3.9	5.4	7.2	9.3	8.1	8.1	8.3	6.8
France	1.7	2.6	4.5	9.0	8.9	8.9	43.6	43.9
Germany	0.6	1.0	3.2	5.9	5.1	5.1	45.0	49.0
Holland	0.8	1.5	4.9	9.7	7.5	6.5	51.0	49.9
Italy	5.1	5.7	6.6	9.5	9.9	11.2	64.6	70.4
Japan	1.2	1.2	1.9	2.5	2.1	2.1	16.1	18.7
Spain	2.4	2.8	5.2	17.5	15.9	16.3	55.4	58.5
Sweden	1.6	2.2	1.9	2.4	1.5	1.5	9.1	6.5
Switzerland	na	na	na	0.8	0.6	0.6	na	na
UK	2.5	3.3	5.0	10.0	6.9	5.9	44.4	40.8
USA	4.2	4.6	6.7	7.2	5.4	5.5	9.1	5.7
EC	2.3	2.9	4.8	9.6	8.4	8.4	52.8	53.7
OECD	2.7	3.2	4.9	7.3	6.1	6.3	33.3	33.7

[a] Those unemployed for 12 months or more as % of total unemployment.
[b] National definitions.

Source: OECD

Total unemployment

Unemployment never drops to zero for various reasons.

- **Frictional unemployment.** There are always people changing jobs and temporarily recorded as unemployed. Their number might be reduced by better information flows (bringing together vacancies and the unemployed) and training.
- **Structural unemployment.** This indicates people whose skills

Figure 5.3

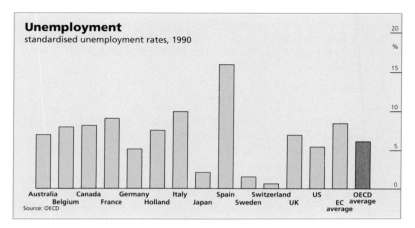

Unemployment
standardised unemployment rates, 1990

Source: OECD

and locations do not match job opportunities, usually because they were trained for industries which are collapsing under competition from modern technology and/or imports. Structural job losses can best be reduced through retraining and improving labour mobility.

- **Seasonal unemployment.** Agriculture, construction and tourism are especially vulnerable to seasonal variation.
- **Residual unemployment.** This is the hard core of people who are virtually unemployable, perhaps due to their inability to integrate with the modern world.

The natural rate

Economists argue that there is a natural rate of unemployment (NRU) or non-accelerating inflation rate of unemployment (NAIRU) at which the demand and supply for labour are in balance.

The basic premise is that an increase in demand can be translated into higher employment only up to the NAIRU, at which point employment stops growing and the higher demand spills over into higher inflation.

Estimates of the NAIRU are subjective and vary from country to country and over time, depending on the level of minimum wages, benefit rates, payroll taxes, unionisation and demographic factors such as the age structure of the labour force.

The cycle

There is a clear cyclical pattern in unemployment. As demand

65

increases, companies take on more workers and unemployment decreases. When there is no more labour available (when the NAIRU is reached), demand bubbles over into inflation or imports. Strong consumer demand is less likely to be inflationary if the unemployment rate is well above the NAIRU rather than close to it.

Longer-term trends

Unemployment in the industrial countries started to rise again in the early 1990s, to an average of 7% of the labour force in 1991 (more than double the average rate of the 1960s). The rate was higher in Europe (9%), and significantly lower in Japan (2%) where jobs-for-life are part of the culture.

The structure of unemployment helps to identify economic problem areas. Long-term unemployment (those unemployed for more than one year) rose to about one-third of total unemployment by the start of the 1990s; although it was lower in Japan (18% of the labour force) and America (6%) where there is more job mobility. In 1990 the average unemployed person had been out of work for ten weeks in America compared with a year in France.

Other clues

The monthly change in unemployment is a good guide to economic developments. Compare the last 2–3 months with the average change in the same period of the previous year. Most figures are seasonally adjusted, but watch out for the effects of severe weather or industrial disputes.

Other figures, such as weekly claims for unemployment benefit, job advertisements for help wanted and vacancies, provide useful back-up to unemployment figures.

Regional unemployment figures provide a guide to structural unemployment since they highlight the relationship between job losses and the location of known twilight industries.

6

FISCAL INDICATORS

"Blessed are the young, for they shall inherit the national debt."
Herbert Hoover

Fiscal indicators are concerned with government revenue and expenditure, which are significant influences on the circular flow of incomes (see page 40). Taxes and duties take money out, while spending is an injection. In any one day or year the American government spends more than any other government, company or other organisation anywhere in the world.

Fiscal activities allow governments to provide services, redistribute incomes and influence the overall level of economic activity. They are one of the government's tools for controlling the economy. Others include monetary policy (see Chapter 12) and direct intervention and controls over wages, prices and industrial activity.

TAX REVENUES

The ratio of total tax revenues to GDP is a measure of a country's tax burden. On that basis, Scandinavian countries top the tax league. Sweden has the highest taxes, equivalent to 57.7% of GDP in 1990, up from 49.1% in 1980. A long way behind, in second and third places, are Denmark (48.1%) and Norway, which was the only country to reduce its tax burden significantly, from 47.1% in 1980 to 46.2% in 1990. Despite the much trumpeted "tax cuts" in the 1980s in America and Britain, the tax burdens of both countries actually increased. Britain's taxes rose from 35.3% of its GDP in 1980 to 36.8% in 1990; America's edged up from 29.5% to 30.1%. America and Australia have the lowest tax burdens among the OECD economies.

The Economist, September 21st 1991

Level of government

Various problems of definition arise because of different treatment of financial transactions by central government, local authorities, publicly owned enterprises, and so on.

In an attempt to standardise, international organisations such as the OECD focus on general government, which covers central and local authorities, separate social security funds where applicable, and province or state authorities in federations such as North America, Australia, Germany, Spain and Switzerland.

Watch out for fiscal fraud: spending can be shifted to publicly owned enterprises which are generally classified as being outside general government. Net lending to such enterprises is part of government spending, but it is not always included in "headline" expenditure figures.

Timing

Many governments run their accounts on a calendar year basis. Britain, Canada and Japan have financial years which cover the 12 months to March 31st; Australia and Sweden's fiscal years run to June 30th; and America's ends on September 30th.

PUBLIC EXPENDITURE

Measures: Spending by the government.
Significance: Affects aggregate demand, size of the budget deficit.
Presented as: Monthly and annual totals in current prices.
Focus on: Total, trends.
Yardstick: OECD average public expenditure was 40.5% of GDP during the 1980s.
Released: Monthly, at least one month in arrears.

The cycle and the automatic stabiliser

Government spending provides services including law and order, defence, education and health, roads, and so on. Such spending is an injection to the circular flow of income and has a considerable effect on aggregate demand. It is a stabilising influence to the extent that payments of welfare benefits increase when unemployment rises, which helps to maintain consumer spending.

Classification

Public spending may be classified in several different ways.

- **By level of government:** central and local authorities, state or provincial authorities for federations, social security funds and public corporations.
- **By department:** agriculture, defence, trade, and so on.
- **By function:** such as environmental services, which might be provided by more than one department.
- **By economic category:** current, capital, and so on.

In order to interpret the economic effect of public spending, its breakdown into current and capital spending is usually most instructive.

Current spending

Major categories of current spending include the following.

- **Pay of public sector employees:** this generally seems to rise faster than other current spending.
- **Other current spending:** on goods and services such as stationery, medicines, uniforms, and so on.
- **Subsidies:** on goods and services such as public housing and agricultural support.
- **Social security:** including benefits for sickness, old age, family allowances, and so on; social assistance grants and unfunded employee welfare benefits paid by general government.
- **Interest on the national debt.**

Interest payments reflect the size of the national debt (see page 78) and the level of interest rates. In the early 1990s interest payments ranged from 2–3% of total public expenditure in Sweden, Finland and Japan, to around 20% in Italy and Belgium.

Social security transfers do not directly create output and are not included when measuring GDP. Their size reflects the level of state support, demographics (see Population, page 57) and the economic cycle. Payments are mostly financed by specific employers' and employees' contributions. Where these are passed through a separate social security budget, "headline" spending figures are lower.

Subsidies are caught in the market price measure of GDP, but are added back in as part of the adjustment to a factor cost basis. They range from less than 1% of GDP in America and Japan to nearly 5% in Sweden.

Other current spending on pay and other goods and services makes up the "government consumption" component of GDP on an expenditure basis. This exceeds 25% of GDP in countries such as Sweden and Denmark where many services are supplied by the government rather than the private sector.

69

Capital spending

Capital spending is mainly fixed investment in infrastructure and dwellings. Note that some spending is arbitrarily classified as current spending even when there is a considerable capital outlay, such as in defence. Also current spending on things such as education, industrial training and research and development might be regarded as investment although they are never classified as such in economic figures.

This capital spending is part of investment in the expenditure measure of GDP. Public sector investment ranges from around 1.5% of GDP in Britain and America to a massive 5% in Japan.

Patterns

Monthly public spending figures are rarely seasonally adjusted, although there is often a definite pattern of spending during the fiscal year. Eliminate this by comparing the latest 2–3 months with the same period 12 months earlier, or the fiscal year to date with the same part of the previous year, but note that the smoothing effect will be smaller at the start of the year (perhaps covering only two months) than the end (when perhaps 11 months are included).

Targets

The year-to-date comparison is useful for judging spending in relation to budget projections. For example, if in the first six months of the fiscal year spending is 5% up from the previous first half and expenditure is projected to rise by 2% during the year as a whole, it is a fair bet that the government is overspending. However, watch for any erratic items which distort the seasonal pattern.

Spending tends to rise above target if the economy grows more slowly than expected. Always ask whether government economic forecasts are realistic when looking at expenditure projections.

Prices

Monthly government spending figures are always presented in nominal money terms. Judge their influence on the real level of economic activity by deflating them. For example, if government consumption rises by 10% and inflation is 6%, the real level of such consumption is 4% higher.

Choosing an appropriate deflator requires care. Table 13.1 (page 183) shows how public sector prices have tended to rise faster than those in the private sector. This "relative price effect" suggests that suppliers have found that public servants will tolerate larger price rises than private individuals.

Quarterly and annual spending figures are available in volume terms. The consumption component can be found in GDP data, although public investment is not usually distinguished separately from private investment in the main GDP breakdowns.

Table 6.1   **General government spending**
As % of GDP, 1960–90

	Final consumption	Social security	Other current[a]	Total current	Total capital[b]	Total outlays
Australia	15.6	7.3	4.4	27.3	3.3	30.6
Belgium	15.0	17.3	8.0	40.3	2.8	43.1
Canada	18.1	9.5	7.2	34.8	3.4	38.2
France	16.7	18.1	5.0	39.8	4.0	43.8
Germany	17.9	14.9	5.4	38.1	4.9	43.0
Holland	15.8	23.6	5.5	44.9	5.2	50.1
Italy	14.7	14.5	8.1	37.4	4.1	41.5
Japan	8.9	7.7	3.5	20.2	6.1	26.3
Spain	11.6	10.6	1.5	23.6	5.5	29.2
Sweden	23.7	14.5	8.0	46.2	4.6	50.8
Switzerland	11.8	10.7	3.3	25.8	0.0	25.8
UK	19.1	10.4	7.3	36.9	4.1	41.0
USA	17.9	8.9	4.1	30.9	1.8	32.6
EC	16.6	14.4	6.4	37.4	4.3	41.7
OECD	16.2	10.9	5.3	32.4	3.3	35.7

[a] Subsidies and interest on the national debt.
[b] Fixed investment and purchases of land and intangible assets.

Source: OECD

Figure 6.1

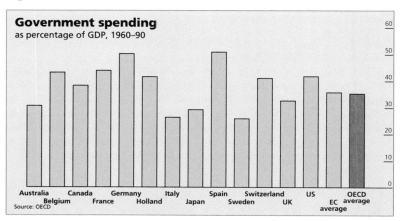

Government spending
as percentage of GDP, 1960–90

Australia   Canada   Germany   Italy   Spain   Switzerland   US   OECD average
Belgium   France   Holland   Japan   Sweden   UK   EC average
Source: OECD

GOVERNMENT REVENUES

Measures: Government receipts mainly from taxes and duties.
Significance: Affects aggregate demand; finances (partly) government spending.
Presented as: Monthly and annual totals in current prices.
Focus on: Total; trends.
Yardstick: Compare with spending (see Budget balance, page 74). OECD receipts averaged 36% of GDP during the 1980s.
Released: Monthly, at least one month in arrears.

Overview

Government revenues are raised largely through taxes, social security contributions, fees or charges for services, and some miscellaneous sources such as interest on government loans. A few governments also conduct trading activities which generate income.

For the industrial countries as a group in the 1980s, personal income taxes, payroll taxes (largely social security) and taxes on spending each accounted for 25–30% of the total tax take. The remaining 16% came mainly from taxes on company profits and property.

Asset sales. One other source of income is receipts from the privatisation of activities previously undertaken by the public sector. In some countries, such as Britain, the receipts are classified as "negative expenditure". Either way, they have a once-off effect on public finances which is perhaps akin to selling the family silver and should not be mistaken for an underlying improvement.

The cycle and the automatic stabiliser

In addition to financing government spending, taxes have a major effect on economic activity.

They also have an important automatic stabilising influence. The government tax take increases and helps to moderate consumer demand when more people are earning and spending more at the top of the economic cycle. Similarly, the tax take declines during recession and to some extent helps to offset falling wage incomes. The change in tax take is more than proportionate since marginal tax rates exceed average tax rates as income rises.

Progressive or regressive

• **Progressive taxes** take a larger proportion of cash from the rich than from the poor, such as income tax where the marginal percentage rate of tax increases as income rises.

- **Proportional taxes** take the same percentage of everyone's income, wealth or expenditure, but the rich pay a larger amount in total.
- **Regressive taxes** take more from the poor. For example, a flat-rate tax of £200, such as Britain's ill-fated poll tax, takes a greater proportion of the income of a lower-paid worker than of a higher-paid worker.

Direct or indirect

Direct taxes. These are levied directly on people or companies. They include taxes on personal and corporate income, capital gains, capital transfers, inheritances and wealth; and royalties on mineral extraction.

Direct taxes are nearly always charged at percentage rates and frequently they are progressive. Payroll taxes tend to be regressive if considered separately from the associated social security benefits.

As mentioned in the previous brief, social security payments are mostly financed by specific employers' and employees' contributions. Where these are passed through a separate social security budget, "headline" revenue figures are lower. On the other hand, Denmark's social security bill is mainly met from general taxation, which depresses the apparent level of social security revenues.

Indirect taxes. These are levied on goods and services and include the following.

- Value-added tax (VAT) charged on the value added at each stage of production; this amounts to a single tax on the final sale price.
- Sales and turnover taxes which may be levied on every transaction (for example, wheat, flour, bread) and cumulate as a product is made.
- Customs duties on imports.
- Excise duties on home-produced goods, sometimes at penal rates to discourage activities such as smoking or drinking alcohol.

Indirect taxes tend to be regressive, as poorer people spend a bigger slice of their income. They are charged at either flat or percentage rates. Flat-rate duties do not rise with inflation and have to be "revalorised", usually in the annual budget, if the government is to retain its real tax-take.

73

GDP at market prices includes indirect taxes, which increase selling prices and have to be subtracted as part of the adjustment to a factor cost basis (see page 34).

Monthly figures

As with spending figures, revenues are usually published monthly in nominal values. Erratic movements can be smoothed out by taking several months together. They can be converted into real terms using the same deflator that is used for public expenditure.

When comparing revenues against budget projections, remember that revenues will tend to be below expectation if the economy grows more slowly than forecast.

BUDGET BALANCE, DEFICIT, SURPLUS (PSBR, PSDR)

Measures: Net total of government spending less revenues in one month/year.
Significance: Indicator of government's fiscal stance.
Presented as: Monthly and annual totals in current prices.
Focus on: Totals; trends.
Yardstick: The average OECD deficit was 3.4% of GDP during the 1980s.
Released: Monthly, at least one month in arrears.

Overview

Balanced budgets (revenues equal spending) sound prudent but may not always be in the best interests of economic management. Perfect balance is hard to achieve anyway, because of the automatic stabilisers in spending and revenue.

Budget deficits (spending exceeds revenues) boost total demand and output through a net injection to the circular flow of incomes. As with personal finances, a deficit on current spending may signal imprudence. However, a deficit to finance capital investment expenditure helps to lay the basis for future output and can be sustained so long as there are private or foreign savings willing to finance it in a non-inflationary way.

Deficits are more common than surpluses. In the 1970s and early 1980s many OECD governments went on a borrowing binge, often with adverse consequences. High levels of government borrowing tend to push up interest rates and so may crowd out private-sector investment. The average budget deficit of OECD countries fell from a peak of 4.2% of GDP in 1983 to 1.1% in

1989, but it has since started to creep up again. Italy's deficit at around 10% of GDP is among the highest in relative terms. Such figures are more usually associated with high-inflation developing countries.

The world's largest deficit in absolute terms is that of America. The federal deficit grew from $74 billion in fiscal 1980 (less than 3% of GDP) to an expected $400 billion for the fiscal year to September 30th 1992 (nearly 6% of American GDP), due to defects in budgetary control and irreconcilable spending and revenue aims.

Budget surpluses (revenues exceed expenditure) may be prudent if a government is building up a large surplus on its social security fund in order to meet an expected increase in its future pensions bill as the population ages. However, a surplus may be undesirable if it takes too much money out of the circular flow.

The world's largest relative budget surpluses (20–30% of GDP) have been run by Kuwait before the 1990 Iraqi invasion and Botswana, which receive large incomes from the sale of oil and diamonds respectively. The receipts come from foreigners rather than the domestic circular flow, so the surpluses manage to stimulate even though they appear deflationary. Other countries' surpluses tend to be smaller, typically up to 5% of GDP.

Tighter or looser. Fiscal policy is said to have tightened if a deficit is reduced or converted into a surplus or if a surplus is increased. A move in the opposite direction is called a loosening of fiscal policy.

The cycle and the automatic stabiliser

There is an automatic stabiliser built into the budget balance. Surpluses reduce or tip into the red and deficits grow during a recession when tax revenues fall and welfare spending increases. This helps to maintain aggregate demand. The opposite happens during an economic boom.

The cyclically adjusted budget balance is the normal balance with cyclical fluctuations removed. This helps to identify the underlying fiscal stance, but such figures should always be regarded with suspicion because it is difficult to get the adjustments right.

Definitions

There are three main ways of looking at the budget balance. One is the published "headline" balance which depends on national definitions and accounting practices. The other two are the borrowing requirement and net savings, both of which are usually tricky to identify precisely from published figures.

The borrowing requirement. The net total of government spending less revenues is the gap which has to be financed by borrowing or which allows debt to be repaid. The announced budget balance in Britain is exactly this figure: the public-sector borrowing requirement (PSBR), or for surpluses the public-sector debt repayment (PSDR).

In most other countries the precise definition varies depending on what is included in "the budget". There are two important areas to consider.

- **Level of government.** Headline budget figures for North America are for federal government only and for France cover just central government. At the other extreme, those for Germany cover federal, Länder and local authorities, and Switzerland's include federal, confederations, cantons and local government.

- **On or off budget.** Many government activities fall outside the normal budget, including lending by government agencies and government farm crop or export insurance, as well as government-guaranteed borrowing by publicly owned enterprises and government-guaranteed lending by private sector bodies. Two other specific examples worthy of note are the American savings and loan rescue plan which was expected to cost over $100 billion in 1991–96, and the German Treuhand agency which among other things was authorised to borrow DM25 billion (about $15 billion) in 1990–91 to help to restructure and privatise east German industry.

Net savings. The balance of current spending and receipts indicates the public sector's net savings; the extent to which the public sector is adding to or subtracting from the circular flow of incomes. This differs from the budget balance in that it includes only current, not capital, transactions.

Monthly figures and targets

Budget balances are usually published monthly in nominal values. Erratic movements can be smoothed by taking several months together. They can be converted into real terms by deflating spending and revenue separately (see previous two briefs).

When comparing cumulative budget balances with projections, remember that deficits tend to expand if the economy grows less slowly than forecast.

Table 6.2 **General government budget balances**
% of GDP

	1960–67	1968–73	1974–79	1980–89	Net public debt[a], 1990
Australia	1.4	1.4	−2.0	−10	na
Belgium	na	na	na	−8.8	120.6
Canada	−0.8	0.7	−1.7	−4.5	40.3
France	0.5	0.5	−1.1	−2.1	25.0
Germany	0.8	0.2	−3.0	−2.1	22.6
Holland	−0.7	−0.5	−2.3	−5.7	62.0
Italy	−1.8	−4.8	−9.2	−11.0	101.4
Japan	1.0	0.9	−3.4	−1.1	4.3
Spain	na	0.4	−0.7	−4.3	30.5
Sweden	3.3	4.4	1.3	−1.1	−6.4
Switzerland	na	na	na	na	na
UK	−1.1	−0.4	−4.1	−1.8	29.4
USA	−0.6	−0.6	−1.4	−2.5	34.5
EC	−0.3	−0.7	−3.6	−4.4	43.1
OECD	−0.2	−0.2	−2.4	−3.4	31.3

[a] EC average covers members listed in this table only; OECD is above countries plus Denmark, Finland and Norway; figures for Germany, France, Holland and Japan exclude corporate shares from financial assets.

Source: OECD

The Reagan years were not kind to those who contended that budget deficits were bad because they hogged, or "crowded out", savings that would otherwise have flowed into productive investment. The notion seemed eminently commonsensical, yet no academic was able to prove it. Though budget deficits grew in seven of President Reagan's eight years, long-term interest rates fell, reducing the nominal cost of capital for investment. And the economy roared.

So it was with a certain *Schadenfreude* that proponents of the crowding-out theory greeted George Bush's willingness after 1989 to see the annual deficits put Mr Reagan's ones to shame. Here, at last, would be proof of crowding out. Record fiscal deficits would drag down an economy that, finding the cost of borrowing too high, would be unable to invest in its own recovery.

There is a flaw in this simple model, and it is called the rest of the world. Foreigners provided lots of capital for the Reagan boom, and are still doing so. Only if they stopped – ie, if the external current-account deficit disappeared – might American interest rates have to jump.

Even so, proponents of the crowding-out theory should not give up yet. There are good reasons why lenders, whether

foreign or domestic, are not taking the budget deficit serious-
ly at the moment, even though it is on course to top $350
billion this year. One reason is the savings-and-loan bail-out.
Though the cost is huge – $70 billion this year [1992] alone –
it is a once-only affair. The total cost has already been discounted. Another reason is that America is, or was until
recently, in recession. Tax revenues are bound to fall; equal-
ly, they are bound to pick up with the economy.

And that is precisely when there may be a problem with
crowding out. Nobody wants to invest during a recession, so
the budget deficit has recently had credit markets to itself.
Come the recovery, everyone will want to borrow: will foreigners again be so obliging? Just servicing the federal debt
costs America $200 billion a year, equivalent to two-thirds
of what it spends on its bloated defence. Hands up those
who think that the capital borrowed by the American government could not be used more productively?

The Economist, January 25th 1992

Figure 6.2

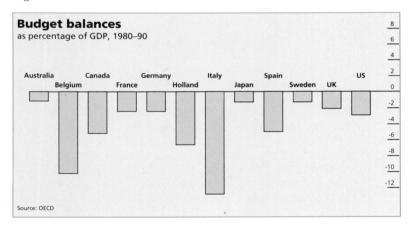

NATIONAL DEBT; GOVERNMENT OR PUBLIC DEBT

Measures: Long-run cumulative total of government spending less rev-
                   enues.
Significance: Inter-generational transfer; interest payments add to borrowing.
Presented as: Annual totals in current prices.
Focus on: Total, particularly as a percentage of GDP; trends.
Yardstick: Varies widely; see text.
Released: Mainly annually; not easily found.

Overview

The public or national debt is the cumulative total of all government borrowing less repayments. It is financed mainly by citizens and may be seen as a transfer between generations. This contrasts with external debt (see page 138) which has to be financed out of export earnings.

Size of debt

Table 6.2 shows the relative size of various national debts in 1990. Belgium and Italy head the list with debt that is greater than their annual GDP.

The debt is often understated since governments carry various liabilities which do not show on their balance sheets. For example, public-sector pensions are usually unfunded, that is, paid out of current income rather than from a reserve created during the individual's working life as happens with private-sector pensions.

Economic theory provides few clues to the optimum ratio of public debt to GDP. Trends over time are often a better measure of a government's creditworthiness than the absolute level of debt. A country with an ever-rising debt ratio, such as Italy, is clearly heading for trouble.

Figure 6.3

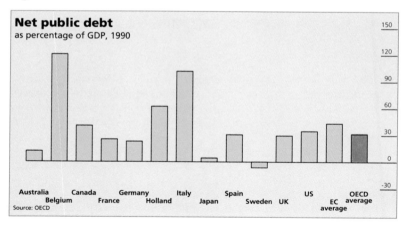

Net public debt
as percentage of GDP, 1990

Australia Canada Germany Italy Spain US OECD average
Belgium France Holland Japan Sweden UK EC average
Source: OECD

7

CONSUMERS

"Live within your income, even if you have to borrow money to do so."
Josh Billings

Overview

Consumers are important since personal consumption accounts for between half and two-thirds of GDP.

In general, if consumers' incomes are boosted (perhaps due to wage rises or tax cuts) they will save some and spend the rest. The part which is spent becomes income for someone else, who in turn spends and saves. The process is repeated and the multiplier effect makes everyone better off, provided that the growth in spending goes into extra production rather than higher prices.

At the same time, the proportion of consumers' income that is saved provides the finance for investment, which is essential for future production, income and consumption.

Consumers, persons and households

For the most part, economic analysis is most effective if focused on a clearly defined group of economic agents, such as households. However, national accounting practices vary and figures are not generally available for such neat units. Terminology can become cloudy.

- **Household.** A group of people living under one roof and sharing cooking facilities.
- **Consumer sector and personal sector.** These terms are generally used interchangeably. They are usually defined to include: households and individuals; owners of unincorporated businesses; non-profit-making bodies serving individuals; private trusts; and private pension, life assurance and welfare funds.
- **Private consumption.** The same as personal consumption since, by national accounts definition, companies do not

consume. But businesses invest, so private (personal plus business) investment is different from personal investment.

- **Total consumption.** Personal (private) consumption plus government consumption.

PERSONAL INCOME, DISPOSABLE INCOME

Measures:	Personal sector total income and income after tax.
Significance:	Basis for consumption and savings.
Presented as:	Money totals.
Focus on:	Growth rates.
Yardstick:	3% a year in real terms.
Released:	Mainly quarterly, monthly in USA; 1–3 months in arrears.

Personal income is current income received by the personal sector from all sources. The bulk is wages and salaries, but the total also covers rents (including the imputed rental value to owner-occupiers of their homes), interest and dividends (including those received by life assurance and pension funds), and current transfers such as social security benefits paid to persons and business donations to charities.

Personal disposable income (PDI). Personal income after the deduction of personal direct taxes and fees (such as passport fees), and current transfers abroad. The figures in Table 7.1 give an indication of the composition of income and disposable income.

Real personal income and PDI. Personal incomes and personal disposable income are occasionally quoted in nominal terms, that is, before allowing for inflation. Real personal income and real PDI are incomes adjusted for inflation. Consumer prices can be used if no other deflator is available. Loosely, if incomes rise by 5% and prices increase by 3%, real incomes are 2% higher.

International comparisons

International comparisons are affected by differences in the provision or treatment of private pensions, life insurance, social security, household interest payments, and current and capital transfers.

In general PDI is reasonably consistent internationally, but personal income is less so. For example, British personal income includes employers' social security contributions and excludes employees' contributions. Both sets of contributions are deducted from personal income to arrive at PDI. In America social insurance

81

Table 7.1 **US personal income, outlays and savings in the USA, 1990** $bn

Wages and salaries	2705
of which:	
Productive enterprises	729
Distribution	637
Services	831
Government	508
Other labour income	258
Proprietors' income[a]	402
of which:	
Farm	50
Non-farm	352
Rental income[a]	7
Interest income	124
Dividends	681
Transfers	695
Less social insurance contributions	−226
Personal income	**4646**
Less taxes, etc	−700
Personal disposable income (PDI)	**3946**
Total deductions	−3767
of which:	
Personal consumption	3658
Interest payments	108
Transfers overseas	1
Personal savings	**179**
Savings ratio (savings as % of PDI)	**4.5%**

[a] With inventory and capital consumption adjustments as appropriate.

Source: US Department of Commerce

payments are excluded from both total income and disposable income. Thus British personal income is inflated slightly relative to that in America, but PDI is on the same social security basis in both countries.

Similarly, personal income in Britain includes net interest receipts. In America income includes interest received on savings but interest paid on loans is treated as part of expenditure. In this case American income and PDI are both inflated relative to Britain's.

Interpretation

Incomes are affected by the economic cycle. In general it is advisable to look for sustainable growth in real incomes – too rapid an increase may be inflationary (see Chapter 13). The main components are as follows.

Income from employment. The major influence on personal income. The total depends mainly on the number of people in employment, hours worked (see Chapter 5) and their pay (see Chapter 13).

Income from self-employment. The next most important component of PDI. Self-employed incomes are linked to the general health of the economy. They will increase when nominal GDP rises.

Interest and dividends. Dividends are sensitive to company profits and the state of the economy, while interest payments obviously move in line with interest rates. When borrowing is high relative to savings, an increase in interest rates can mean a fall in net interest income. Generally an increase in interest rates boosts PDI because in most countries (Britain is the main exception) the personal sector has more assets with adjustable interest rates than liabilities.

Taxes and benefits. Changes in the rates of tax or benefits have a rapid effect on PDI (but not, of course, on personal income). The magnitude will depend on the nature of the change; see Chapter 6.

CONSUMER AND PERSONAL EXPENDITURE, PRIVATE CONSUMPTION

Measures:	Spending by persons.
Significance:	Key component of GDP.
Presented as:	Money totals.
Focus on:	Growth rates.
Yardstick:	The OECD average growth in consumer expenditure was 2.8% a year during the 1980s.
Released:	Quarterly with GDP figures, monthly in USA; frequently revised.

Overview

Consumer expenditure is personal (mainly household) spending on goods and services. Thus it includes imputed rents on owner-occupied dwellings; the outlays which would be required to buy income in kind; and administrative costs of life assurance and pension funds. It excludes interest payments; the purchase of land and buildings; transfers abroad; all business expenditure; and spending on second-hand goods, which reflects a transfer of ownership rather than new production.

Strictly speaking, expenditure takes place when goods are purchased, while consumption may take place over several years. For example, the benefit derived from a car or television is enjoyed (consumed) over several years. In practice it is hard to measure consumption and the term is used loosely to mean expenditure. Thus consumer expenditure, personal expenditure and private consumption are all the same thing.

Significance

Spending by consumers accounts for between half and two-thirds of GDP. Arithmetically a 1% rise in consumer expenditure contributes to around a 0.6% increase in total GDP all else being equal, which it rarely is of course. In particular some of the extra consumer spending will go into higher imports.

Spending decisions

Personal income is either spent or saved. Decisions about consumption are intertwined with decisions about savings (see next brief).

The best guesses at what determines spending and saving are the broadly similar "permanent-income hypothesis" and "life-cycle hypothesis", which suggest that consumption is linked to income over a lifetime. Young and old households have a high propensity to spend their income, while those in mid-life save for retirement. In addition, households tend to run down savings or borrow to maintain consumption during a recession (spreading spending over their lifetimes).

Major influences on the level of consumption include the following.

- **Incomes.** In general higher personal incomes allow more spending.
- **Price expectations.** Experience shows that consumers tend to save more (and spend less) during periods of high inflation (see next brief). They may bring spending forward, however, if they expect a one-off increase in prices due to inflation or higher indirect (sales) taxes.
- **Interest rates.** Higher interest rates push up the cost of existing loans and discourage borrowing and, perhaps, encourage savings, all of which depress spending. Nevertheless higher interest rates also redistribute income from young mortgage payers to their elders whose deposits are greater than their borrowings and who may spend their additional interest income.
- **Consumer credit.** More readily available consumer credit may

encourage borrowing, which translates directly into higher spending.

- **Wealth.** A rise in asset values, such as share or house prices, may make consumers feel wealthier and inclined to spend more.
- **Stock level and price of durables.** Consumers tend to regard durables such as cars and electrical appliances as wealth. A sudden end to a period of restricted supply of durables as in eastern Germany in 1990, or a fall in their prices, may encourage a temporary consumer boom. This may set up replacement cycles, with bouts of spending on durables every few years.
- **Social factors.** These may encourage saving to allow bequests or retirement spending.

Figure 7.1

Figure 7.2

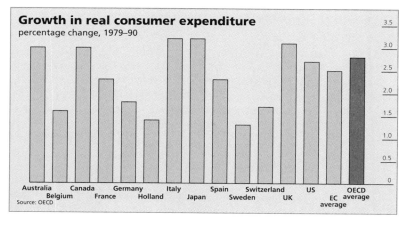

85

Table 7.2 **Consumer expenditure**

	% of GDP 1960–90	Real annual % change 1960–68	1968–73	1973–79	1979–89	1990
Australia	60.0	4.4	5.1	3.0	3.1	2.3
Belgium	63.4	3.5	5.6	2.9	1.5	2.6
Canada	58.2	4.5	5.6	4.4	3.2	1.3
France	59.3	5.4	5.0	2.9	2.2	3.1
Germany	56.0	4.4	5.6	3.2	1.5	4.7
Holland	59.3	5.9	5.2	4.0	1.1	3.9
Italy	60.4	6.3	5.6	3.7	3.2	2.7
Japan	57.0	9.0	8.4	3.9	3.1	4.0
Spain	65.0	7.6	6.4	2.7	2.2	3.7
Sweden	54.3	3.7	2.8	1.8	1.5	–0.3
Switzerland	60.7	4.5	4.8	0.7	1.7	1.5
UK	62.7	2.6	3.6	1.3	3.3	1.0
USA	63.9	4.3	4.0	2.9	2.9	0.9
EC	60.4	4.8	5.1	2.8	2.4	3.1
OECD	61.3	4.9	5.0	3.0	2.8	2.4

Source: OECD

The cycle

There is a cyclical pattern in consumer expenditure. The most volatile component is spending on durables: goods with a life of over one year such as washing machines, furniture and cars.

When economic conditions are tight, spending on durables can be cut more readily than spending on non-durables such as food and heating. Thus there is a stable core of spending on non-durables, and a fluctuating level of spending on durables which moves in line with the economic cycle.

International comparisons

Total spending is affected by the level of services provided by the state. For example, in Belgium and France where health care is initially paid for by the user, the outlays are included in consumer expenditure. Where health services are more or less free at the point of use, as in Britain and Nordic countries, no entry appears under consumer spending. In developing countries a greater proportion of spending is on essentials such as food.

Interpretation

The focus should be on real percentage change. Some countries, such as America, publish monthly figures in nominal terms, which may be deflated by consumer prices to obtain a feel for the real growth. For example, if nominal personal spending grows by 6% and consumer prices rise by 4%, spending has risen by about 2% in real terms. Changes in spending on durables can be an early signal of developments.

Retail sales (page 117), car sales (page 111) and consumer confidence (page 89) also provide leading indicators of spending patterns.

PERSONAL AND HOUSEHOLD SAVINGS; SAVINGS RATIO

Measures: Savings by households.
Significance: Key component of total national savings.
Presented as: Money totals and as a percentage of disposable income.
Focus on: Trends.
Yardstick: The OECD average savings ratio was about 10.3% during the 1980s.
Released: Quarterly or annually; frequently revised.

Overview

Personal savings, an important chunk of national savings (see page 98), are personal disposable income less personal consumption. Many governments also produce savings data for households alone. The household savings ratio is household savings as a percentage of household disposable income.

The household or personal sector's financial deficit or surplus (the net balance of deposits and loans) is different from savings. For this reason consumer borrowing – which influences spending and saving – can be considered separately (see page 84).

International comparisons

Household savings ratios are shown with national savings in Table 8.3. Household savings ratios vary widely between countries. For example, in 1990 net household savings were 4.6% of household disposable income in America and 14.3% in Japan. There are a number of reasons for this.

As far as definitions are concerned, the calculations depend on the treatment of consumer durables, private pensions and life insurance payments, social security, household interest payments, capital transfers and depreciation. Adjusting for such factors reduces the gap between Japan's and America's savings ratios by around 3 percentage points.

Other factors which account for a large part of the remaining

87

Figure 7.3

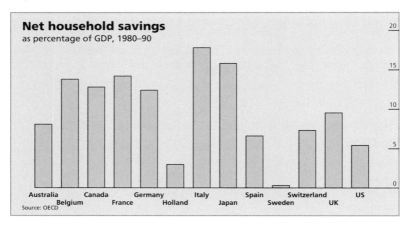

difference between the Japanese and American ratios include the age structure of the population and the labour force; the distribution of incomes; the availability of consumer credit; the tax treatment of savings; the social security system; and economic variables such as those discussed below.

Influences on household savings

The experience of the industrial countries in the 1970s and 1980s highlights some major factors which affect savings. It should be noted that savings appear to be relatively unaffected by changes in interest rates.

The 1970s. Economists were confounded by the rise in savings which accompanied the high inflation of the 1970s. Theory said that with falling real disposable incomes and negative real interest rates the savings ratio should have fallen. It seems that households save more during high inflation in order to maintain the real value of their savings.

The 1980s. Savings ratios fell in the 1980s for several reasons. There was lower inflation; stockmarkets were rising; in some countries higher house prices boosted personal wealth and so encouraged spending; financial liberalisation made borrowing easier; public pensions improved; and the population was ageing (older people save less).

Interpretation

See National savings, page 98, for hints on interpretation. Note that the ageing population (see Population, page 57) is likely to reduce savings rates in Japan and Europe in the 1990s and in North America in the next century.

CONSUMER CONFIDENCE

Measures: Consumers' perception of their economic well-being.
Significance: Determines short-term spending/borrowing/savings plans.
Presented as: Usually index numbers.
Focus on: Trends.
Yardstick: Watch for changes in direction.
Released: Monthly, one month in arrears.

Overview

Survey evidence of consumer perceptions is valuable as a leading indicator. In general, the more optimistic consumers are, the more likely they are to spend money. This boosts consumer spending and economic output. Moreover, consumer confidence makes the government popular and helps to win elections; it is therefore an implicit target of government policy.

Surveys of consumer confidence are conducted by private sector organisations such as the Conference Board in America and Gallup in Britain. The results are presented in index form or as percentage balances (the percentage of consumers feeling more optimistic less the percentage feeling less optimistic). Trends in such indices provide a guide to future economic developments and policies.

Other indicators

Other popular indicators of consumer confidence include the following.

- The misery index I. The rate of consumer-price inflation plus the unemployment rate.
- The misery index II. The rate of consumer-price inflation plus annual interest rates.

In each case the higher the number, the more miserable consumers are assumed to be.

8

INVESTMENT AND SAVINGS

*"Saving is a very fine thing. Especially when your parents have
done it for you."*
Sir Winston Churchill

Overview

Investment deserves special attention because it is so important
for the future health of an economy. It lays the basis for future
production.

Investment is spending on physical assets with a life of more
than one year. This should be distinguished from financial transactions which are known as investment in everyday language but
which are – from an economic viewpoint – savings.

It is conventional to say that businesses invest while individuals
consume. If a household buys itself a personal computer, this is
recorded in the national accounts as personal consumption. If a
business buys the same model, the spending is classed as investment. The rationale is that the household uses a PC for "pleasure"
while a business uses it in the production of future output. A
company's stocks of raw materials and goods are classed as
investment.

The circular flow of incomes

Chapter 4 (page 40) outlined the concept of the circular flow of
incomes. Savings and investment are perhaps the most important
leakage and injection. It is easiest to understand their significance
through an example.

Imagine a simple system in which firms produce $100m of
goods a year. Suppose that households save $20m. Output is
$100m, incomes are $100m, and consumption is $80m. Since the
firms sell only $80m of their output, the remainder is left in stock
at the end of the year. The $20m increase in stocks is classed as
investment spending. In order to meet their wage bills, the firms
have to borrow $20m from the banks where the households saved
their $20m. Output is $100m, incomes are $100m, and total

Table 8.1 **Investment and savings**
% of GDP

	1967–73	1974–79	1980–90
Canada			
Private saving	19.9	22.6	23.8
Government saving	3.0	0.1	−3.5
Foreign saving	0.1	1.9	1.0
Total investment/saving	23.0	24.6	21.3
France			
Private saving	21.3	21.7	18.8
Government saving	4.8	2.9	1.4
Foreign saving	0.7	0.1	0.6
Total investment/saving	26.8	24.7	20.8
Germany			
Private saving	21.5	20.1	20.8
Government saving	5.3	2.4	1.9
Foreign saving	−1.4	−1.0	−2.2
Total investment/saving	25.5	21.5	20.6
Italy			
Private saving	28.3	30.9	28.1
Government saving	−1.2	−5.3	−6.4
Foreign saving	−1.5	0.2	0.9
Total investment/saving	25.6	25.8	22.6
Japan			
Private saving	30.3	29.0	26.3
Government saving	7.7	4.0	5.6
Foreign saving	−1.1	−0.3	−2.0
Total investment/saving	36.9	32.7	29.9
UK			
Private saving	13.3	16.9	15.4
Government saving	6.9	2.2	1.9
Foreign saving	−0.3	0.9	0.2
Total investment/saving	19.9	20.0	17.5
USA			
Private saving	16.6	17.8	16.1
Government saving	−0.6	−1.2	−2.5
Foreign saving	−0.1	nil	1.9
Total investment/saving	15.9	16.6	15.5

Note: Totals may not equal the sum of components due to rounding.

Source: IMF

spending is $80m consumption plus $20m investment which equals $100m.

The leakage of $20m for saving is matched by an injection of $20m for investment. Investment (in stocks or fixed assets) can take place only when some consumption is deferred. By definition, investment = savings.

Of course there is no automatic mechanism which ensures that the amount that households wish to save matches the amount that firms wish to invest. Investment and savings are each determined by different factors which are discussed in the following briefs.

Economic effects of imbalance. Loosely, if planned savings exceed planned investment, stocks pile up and companies cut back their production: GDP falls. If planned savings are less than planned investment, companies produce more to meet the extra demand and GDP rises. (See Cyclical indicators, page 51.)

The golden rule. It is difficult to identify the ideal level of saving and investment. Less saving means more consumption today but less investment and so less future consumption. Economists talk about the "golden rule" which maximises the consumption per head of all generations. Significantly, an IMF study suggests that America's national savings in the period 1986–90 were only half the amount required by the golden rule.

National savings and investment. All sectors of the economy save and invest. Real life is not as simple as business investment and household savings. Table 8.1 shows flows of funds in the seven largest economies. The following briefs discuss the topics in more detail.

FIXED INVESTMENT AND GDFCF

Measures:	Spending on goods with a life of more than one year.
Significance:	Contributes directly to GDP, lays basis for future output.
Presented as:	Value, volume and index numbers.
Focus on:	Volume trend.
Yardstick:	OECD average fixed investment grew by 3.2% a year during the 1980s.
Released:	Quarterly, 1–3 months in arrears; frequently revised.

Overview

Fixed investment is spending on physical assets. Total investment is fixed investment plus investment in stocks of raw materials and goods (see Stocks, page 96).

Physical assets include infrastructure such as roads and docks; buildings such as dwellings, factories and offices; plant and machinery; vehicles; and equipment such as computers. These generally provide the potential for higher output in the future. The economic (as opposed to the social) benefit of dwellings and some infrastructure is more arguable, but most infrastructure boosts economic efficiency. For example, new roads help to get delivery teams back for more work rather than crawling at 10kph through the world's congested cities.

Investment and consumption. By convention, only businesses invest. All personal spending is consumption for national accounts purposes, except the purchase of new dwellings. These have such a long life that they are classed as investment. Most government spending, including that on defence equipment, is classified as consumption (see pages 31–32).

GDFCF. Economists pompously call new investment in physical assets "gross domestic fixed capital formation". Gross because it is before depreciation; domestic because it is at home rather than overseas; fixed because it does not include stocks; and capital formation since it distinguishes physical from financial investment.

Fixed investment is rarely shown net because of the problem of accounting for capital retirements and obsolescence.

Interpretation

Fixed investment accounts for an average of around 20% of GDP in industrial economies. So as a crude rule of thumb, a 1% rise in fixed investment adds around 0.2% to GDP in the same period, all else being constant.

The potential for future output will also be boosted (see Productivity, pages 49–51), especially by investment in plant and machinery. Table 8.2 shows that this is typically 8–9% of GDP.

The direct relationship between investment and output is complex. Investment is shown gross and the increase in productive capacity will be less after allowing for depreciation, and so on, but in developing countries at least, a given change in investment this year can be used as the basis for a moderately reliable forecast of the change in GDP next year.

The cycle. Investment is highly cyclical. Firms are more likely to invest if they are operating at a high level of capacity, if they expect demand to remain high and if interest rates are low. (See Capacity use and Business conditions, pages 107 and 103.) When these conditions are reversed, businesses are likely to cut back on fixed investment. However, investment projects have long lead times and a cut in new investment does not automatically imply a fall in total investment spending.

A 1% increase in demand may be translated into a greater than 1% increase in output if firms respond by increasing investment spending. (See "accelerator principle" in Cyclical indicators, page 51.)

93

Figure 8.1

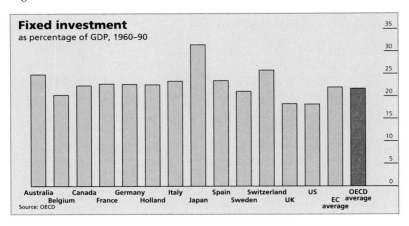

Table 8.2 **Fixed investment**

	As % of gdp, 1960–90				Annual % change in real fixed investment			
	Machinery & equipment	Construction non-res'l	resid-ential	Total	1960–68	1968–73	1973–79	1979–89
Australia	11.3	8.1	5.3	24.8	5.9	4.4	1.2	4.2
Belgium	7.6	7.1	5.2	20.2	5.6	4.4	1.5	1.9
Canada	7.4	9.1	5.9	22.3	5.4	5.5	5.1	5.1
France	8.8	6.7	7.1	22.7	8.0	6.8	0.1	1.9
Germany	8.6	7.4	6.6	22.6	3.1	5.5	0.5	1.4
Holland	9.9	7.1	5.5	22.5	7.7	1.7	−0.1	1.9
Italy	9.9	6.3	7.1	23.3	5.0	4.1	0.4	2.4
Japan	12.3	12.8	6.3	31.4	15.2	12.5	1.5	5.3
Spain	8.9	8.3	5.8	23.4	12.5	7.2	−1.3	4.3
Sweden	7.7	8.2	5.1	21.0	5.4	2.7	−0.6	3.7
Switzerland	9.0	16.8[a]	na	25.7	5.0	6.5	−2.9	5.1
UK	8.5	5.9	3.8	18.2	6.3	2.0	0.2	3.7
USA	7.5	6.0	4.7	18.1	5.0	3.7	1.9	2.6
EC	8.9	6.9	6.0	21.9	6.1	5.0	0.1	2.3
OECD	8.7	7.5	5.6	21.6	6.5	5.8	1.2	3.2

[a] Including residential construction.

Source: **OECD**

Government intervention. Government incentives for investment should be treated with caution as they can be counterproductive in the long run. Tax subsidies make poor investment projects viable.

Figure 8.2

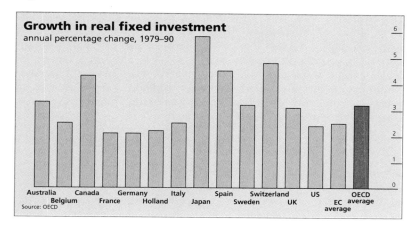

Changes in government investment spending should also be scrutinised. In more mature economies government expenditure can crowd out private-sector investment with detrimental effects, but in developing countries public and private investment are often complementary.

Other indicators. GDP investment figures are released with a lag. Other indicators should be used for advance signals, especially investment intentions, construction spending, housing starts, auto sales, manufacturing production and imports of capital goods.

Sectoral. Investment is classified by ownership rather than end-use. Sectoral investment figures should not be taken at face value. Investment by service companies may reflect spending on goods which are subsequently leased to industrial firms.

INVESTMENT INTENTIONS

Measures: Plans for capital spending, sometimes just in manufacturing.
Significance: Investment adds to current and future GDP.
Presented as: Value, volume totals or changes.
Focus on: Trend: planned volume increases.
Yardstick: Look for planned increases of several percentage points.
Released: Monthly, one month in arrears.

Overview

Governments and trade associations such as the US National Association of Purchasing Managers and the Confederation of British Industry publish the results of surveys of investment intentions. These may be wholly subjective ("Do you expect more or fewer capital authorisations over the next 12 months?") or misleadingly quantitative ("How many dollars' worth of capital spending will you undertake in the calendar year?"). See also Business conditions, page 103.

Value and volume

Where surveys are in value terms, the first step should be to consider how closely the figures relate to volumes. Respondents tend to indicate the value of investment after allowing for any expected price increases, so the totals should be deflated to arrive at the planned volume increase. As a crude deflator use producer prices. If these are rising by 5% and companies expect the value of their investment to increase by 7%, the volume of investment will be about 2% greater. If inflation is accelerating or decelerating, use the consensus view (at the time of the survey) of expected inflation for the period ahead.

Outcomes

Intentions are rarely turned into spending on a one-for-one basis. Investment intentions surveys tell you something about future trends in the economy, but at the same time you should interpret the survey results in the light of developments in the economy. For example, a rise in interest rates after a survey may lead to a lower than announced level of investment.

STOCKS (INVENTORIES)

Measures: Stocks held by producers and distributors.
Significance: Indicator of demand pressures; potential sales.
Presented as: Value and volume totals and changes.
Focus on: Totals in relation to sales, changes.
Yardstick: See text.
Released: Quarterly, sometimes monthly, 1–3 months in arrears; frequently revised.

Overview

Stocks or inventories are materials and fuel, work-in-progress and finished goods held by companies.
The book value of stocks changes for two reasons.

- **Stock appreciation** is an increase in the money value of stocks due to inflation. It adds to nominal income (the inventories can be sold at a profit) but there is no addition to real output.
- **Stockbuilding** (or destocking) is a change in the physical volume of inventories. It reflects the production of goods and affects nominal and real output.

Data are generally collected in value terms and deflated into volume terms using assumptions about accounting practices, stockholding patterns and price changes. The breakdown between the physical change and stock appreciation can be unreliable, especially during periods of rapid inflation.

Cycles

In general the level of stocks rises as national income increases, but there are wide fluctuations which reflect the economic cycle.
Stocks are a buffer between production and consumption. When demand increases unexpectedly, the first sign is a decrease in inventories before manufacturers can respond by increasing output. Alternatively, if an increase in demand is expected, stocks may be built up in advance ready to meet the extra demand. Either way, production can increase faster than demand for short periods during restocking or stockbuilding.
Stocks accumulate when demand turns down unexpectedly; production might fall faster than sales as excess stocks are consumed.

Inflation. Stocks of raw materials react violently to expected changes in world commodity prices (see also Commodity prices, page 190).

Interpretation

The stocks:sales ratios at each stage of activity (manufacturing, wholesaling, retailing) are important leading indicators.
If the ratios are higher than normal (look at a long run of figures), this implies that production and imports will be cut unless demand increases. If the ratios are lower than normal the implication is that production and imports will rise unless demand falls

(but note that stock ratios fell sharply in the industrial countries during the 1980s because of better stock control techniques such as just-in-time). If the ratios are low and there are capacity constraints (high capacity utilisation and/or low unemployment), the excess demand might go into higher inflation or imports.

High or low stocks:sales ratios all the way through the economy give fairly clear signals. Different ratios at different stages imply bottlenecks or structural problems. For example, a low ratio in retailing and a high ratio in manufacturing may indicate that an increase in consumer demand has not yet fed through to manufacturers, or it might suggest that domestic producers cannot provide the required goods and the excess consumer demand is going into imports.

Surveys (see Business conditions, page 103) provide useful evidence about companies' perceptions of their stocks. If, say, manufacturers think that their stocks are too high, they will cut production over the next few months unless demand increases.

GDP

It is not the total level of stocks but the change in the rate of stockbuilding which affects the GDP expenditure measure. An increase in stocks reflects extra output that has not been consumed. Note, however, that a fall in the level of stocks can lead to an increase in GDP if the rate of destocking slows.

The effects of changes in stocks are very limited when measured over several years, but stockbuilding is highly volatile quarter-by-quarter. Accordingly, changes in the rate of stockbuilding can be a major influence on demand and GDP. The snag is that stockbuilding is the trickiest component of GDP to forecast.

NATIONAL SAVINGS, SAVINGS RATIO

Measures: Total savings in an economy.
Significance: Major influence on investment and interest rates.
Presented as: Totals; percentage of GDP.
Focus on: Trends.
Yardstick: The OECD average was 21% during the 1980s.
Released: Quarterly with GDP figures. Total savings = investment.

Overview

Savings (deferred consumption) affect investment (the basis for future output and consumption). For the economy as a whole it is the national savings rate which is important: the sum of savings by the private sector and the government.

Gross savings are the savings required to finance gross investment. Net savings are those required to finance investment net of capital consumption. The national savings ratio is savings as a percentage of GDP.

Private savings

Private savings are the sum of savings by persons and companies. (See also Personal savings, page 86.) Company savings are cyclical since businesses hold liquid reserves to cushion themselves against the economic cycle and to provide funds for expansion.

Government savings

Government savings are general government revenue less current expenditure. Government capital spending is classed as investment. Thus, although the budget balance is often taken as a proxy for government savings, there can be a large difference between the two (amounting to, for example, 4.5% of GDP for Italy during the 1980s).

Government savings or, frequently, dissavings reflect political decisions and are largely cyclical. Budget cuts in the industrial countries are likely to lead to higher government savings or lower government dissavings as a percentage of GDP in the 1990s, especially in America (probably), Canada, Germany and Italy.

National savings and the investment gap

A net inflow of foreign capital implies that domestic savings are less than domestic investment: foreigners' excess savings fill the gap. A net outflow of capital implies that domestic savings are bigger than domestic investment. Net foreign savings are conveniently defined as the balance on the current account of the balance of payments with the sign reversed (see Current account, page 133).

Current-account deficits indicate the extent to which domestic investment is financed by foreign savings. For example, the American current-account deficit (averaging 1.9% of GDP in 1980–90) represented a net inflow of foreign savings of the same proportion.

Interpretation

Trends in domestic savings are an important indicator to watch. The comments in this chapter suggest that an increase in domestic savings rates would be no bad thing. Lower budget deficits, especially for America, would reduce demands on world savings.

Table 8.3   **Savings ratios**

	Households[a]				National[b]			
	1960–67	68–73	74–79	80–90	1960–67	68–73	74–79	80–90
Australia	9.8	11.8	12.6	8.1	24.2	25.6	22.7	19.8
Belgium	12.7	16.1	16.9	13.8	22.3	25.1	21.6	16.7
Canada	5.9	7.5	12.4	12.8	21.3	22.2	22.6	20.1
France	12.2	14.1	15.5	14.2	26.3	27.1	24.9	20.3
Germany	10.3	13.6	13.3	12.4	27.3	27.1	22.6	22.8
Holland	13.8	14.7	13.5	3.0	27.2	27.0	23.0	22.2
Italy	17.3	19.5	22.3	17.8	28.3	28.9	25.7	21.8
Japan	15.2	18.0	21.6	15.8	33.6	38.5	32.8	31.8
Spain	8.9	10.8	10.1	6.6	24.8	26.4	23.9	20.8
Sweden	6.7	4.0	4.2	0.3	24.3	22.9	19.5	17.0
Switzerland	11.6	14.2	11.9	7.3	29.9	32.1	27.7	30.0
UK	5.6	5.1	6.4	9.5	18.2	19.8	16.8	16.6
USA	8.2	9.5	9.6	5.4	19.9	19.6	19.8	16.5
EC	10.9	13.0	14.2	11.8	24.6	25.4	22.5	20.4
OECD	9.7	11.7	13.0	10.3	23.1	24.4	22.8	20.6

[a] Net household savings as % of disposable household income.
[b] Gross national savings as % of GDP.

Source: OECD

Figure 8.3

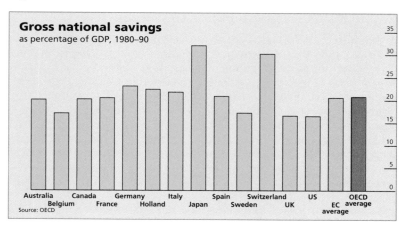

Gross national savings
as percentage of GDP, 1980–90

Australia   Canada   Germany   Italy   Spain   Switzerland   US   OECD
Belgium   France   Holland   Japan   Sweden   UK   EC average
Source: OECD

9

INDUSTRY AND COMMERCE

"If economists were any good at business, they would be rich men instead of advisers to rich men."
Kirk Kerkorian

Partly for historical reasons, there is an abundance of economic indicators relating to industry and commerce in general and manufacturing in particular. These provide useful, timely signals of activity, but it should be borne in mind that their coverage is relatively narrow.

Interpretation

Industrial and commercial indicators provide a guide to both the output and expenditure measures of GDP. These should be used in conjunction with cyclical indicators (page 51) to assess overall economic activity.

Output. The main clues to output include manufacturing and industrial production, car production and sales, construction spending, housing starts and wholesale and retail sales.

Table 9.1 shows the relative importance of the main sectors. Note that services account for 60–70% of output in the major industrialised countries, but they are relatively neglected among the commonly followed indicators of output. Employment (page 61), consumer spending (page 83) and government consumption (page 31) also provide clues to services.

It is "value added" that matters – the value of output less the cost of raw materials and other inputs. This is what manufacturing and industrial production figures measure, but the other indicators are before the deduction of input costs.

Expenditure. The main indicators of industrial and commercial expenditure are fixed investment and investment in stocks (see Chapter 8).

Fixed investment figures are available only after a lag. This chapter will show that business conditions, construction spending

101

and housing starts provide a useful advance guide; so do manufacturers' production of capital goods and net imports of capital goods. Manufacturing, wholesale and retail inventories provide clues to changes in total stocks.

Investment figures should be used with consumer spending, government consumption and exports and imports to assess total GDP on an expenditure basis. This chapter's briefs on retail and vehicle sales provide clues to consumer spending and imports. Manufacturers' orders from abroad are indicative of export demand.

Coverage

Many figures such as orders and productivity can be related to the whole economy, but for convenience are often produced for manufacturing alone. It is important to be clear about the coverage of any figures you use. Where they relate to manufacturing alone, consider whether other sectors of the economy might be moving differently.

Key indicators

The following briefs are arranged broadly from top to bottom: from the whole economy through to individual sectors, and from manufacturing through wholesaling to retailing.

Table 9.1 **Output by sector**

	% of GDP, 1990[a]				Real annual % growth, 1960–89			
	Agri-culture	Ind-ustry	Manu-factrg	Serv-ices	Agri-culture	Ind-ustry	Manu-factrg	Serv-ices
Australia	4	32	15	64	3.1	3.7	3.1	4.3
Belgium	2	31	22	67	1.2	3.5	4.1	3.4
Canada	3	30	17	67	1.5	3.6	4.0	4.9
France	3	29	21	67	1.6	3.8	4.1	4.1
Germany	2	37	32	62	1.3	2.5	2.9	3.5
Holland	4	31	20	65	3.6	3.4	4.0	3.3
Italy	4	34	22	63	1.3	4.3	5.4	4.1
Japan	3	41	30	56	0.1	8.1	9.3	6.2
Spain	5	9	18	86	2.1	5.7	5.7	4.5
Sweden	3	34	23	63	1.3	2.9	2.9	3.0
Switzerland	4	35	26	61	na	na	na	na
UK	2	37	20	62	2.6	1.5	1.4	3.2
USA	2	29	17	69	1.4	2.7	3.5	3.7
EC	3	33	24	64	1.8	3.1	3.5	3.8
OECD	5	43	32	54	1.5	3.6	4.2	4.0

[a] Or most recent year available.

Sources: OECD; World Bank

Figure 9.1

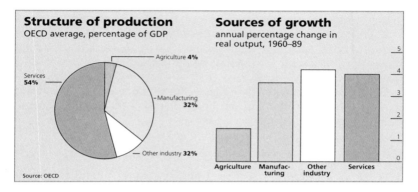

Structure of production
OECD average, percentage of GDP

Agriculture **4%**
Services **54%**
Manufacturing **32%**
Other industry **32%**
Source: OECD

Sources of growth
annual percentage change in real output, 1960–89

Agriculture | Manufac-turing | Other industry | Services

BUSINESS CONDITIONS; INDICES AND SURVEYS

Measures: Anecdotal evidence of business climate.
Significance: Valuable early warning of changes in economic cycle.
Presented as: Index number or percentage balance of companies optimistic or pessimistic.
Focus on: Trends.
Yardstick: Watch for indicators of rising or falling confidence. The US NAPM index has a breakpoint of 50 (see text).
Released: Monthly or quarterly, one month in arrears; rarely revised.

Overview

Surveys provide valuable evidence of perceptions and expectations relating to business conditions, usually in manufacturing. Responses are subjective but they give early signals of changes in economic trends. (See briefs on Orders, Inventories, Prices, Retail sales, and so on, for comments on individual parts of the surveys.) Private-sector bodies conduct surveys in some countries (for example, confederations of industry in Australia, Britain, Finland; IFO in Germany), but some government agencies do the work (for example, Statistics Canada, the Bank of Japan). Many surveys are quarterly, although where they are monthly some questions are asked only 3–4 times a year (for example, capacity use in France and Germany). Two of the most widely watched surveys are described below. Other surveys follow similar patterns.

America

The US National Association of Purchasing Managers (NAPM)

103

publishes monthly indices covering factors such as the state of order books, inventories, production and prices, and a composite index of industrial conditions.

A composite index reading above 50 indicates an expanding manufacturing sector, a figure below that indicates a contracting manufacturing sector. A reading below 44 is taken as a sign of a declining economy overall.

Also useful are the US Federal Reserve's report on regional trends (known as the tan or beige book) and the Conference Board's surveys of business conditions.

Britain

The Confederation of British Industry (CBI) conducts several surveys. Its monthly and quarterly surveys of about 1,250 industrial companies provide guides to manufacturers' expectations, mostly for the four months ahead. Its monthly surveys of 500 distributors, conducted in association with the *Financial Times*, provide information about current and expected conditions in 15,000 retailing and wholesaling outlets.

The CBI surveys are presented in percentage balance form (that is, the percentage balance of companies reporting orders up less the percentage balance reporting them down). The OECD uses a similar style. Interpretation is not as clear-cut as with the NAPM surveys, but trends provide a good indication of perceived conditions.

The CBI confidence measure is reckoned to provide a guide to corporate earnings nine months in advance.

BUSINESS CONFIDENCE

According to Dun & Bradstreet's latest survey of sales expectations, businessmen in several countries are feeling cheerier. Comparing optimists and pessimists, a net 52% of American businessmen expect sales to rise in the second quarter of this year, up from 40% in the first quarter. In Britain optimists outweigh pessimists by 25% up from only 7%. But business confidence in Japan has slumped for the seventh consecutive quarter; a net 3% now expect lower sales, compared with a net 12% who predicted a rise in the first quarter and a 1990 peak of 84% expecting higher sales. The most dramatic swing is in New Zealand, where a net 57% now expect sales to rise. Fingers crossed, economic recovery may at last be on its way.

The Economist, May 2nd 1992
(see also Figure on next page)

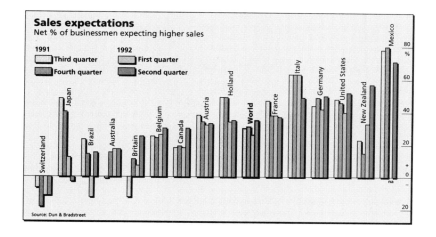

INDUSTRIAL AND MANUFACTURING PRODUCTION

Measures: Value-added output of mines and manufacturing companies.
Significance: Indicator of industrial activity.
Presented as: Index numbers in volume terms.
Focus on: Trends in volume terms.
Yardstick: OECD average manufacturing production grew by 2.8% a year during the 1980s; industrial production grew by 2.4%.
Released: Monthly, at least one month in arrears; revised.

Coverage

There are two main series, which are usually released together.

- **Manufacturing production.** This is the value-added output of manufacturing companies. Some countries such as Italy and Spain include mining and quarrying.
- **Industrial production.** This is manufacturing production plus the supply of energy and water, and the output of mines, oil wells, and quarries. It generally excludes agriculture, trade, transport, finance and all other services.

National coverage varies widely. Canada includes services relating to mineral extraction; Germany covers construction; Portugal leaves out clothing, furniture and printing; Sweden excludes utilities; Switzerland omits mining and quarrying.

In total, the index in Japan covers about 60% of industry, Spain around 70%, Germany and Italy 80%, and Holland, Sweden and

105

Britain up to 100%. France conducts a monthly survey covering 65% and a fuller quarterly survey covering 85% of industry. Australia and Switzerland have quarterly indices only.

The importance of manufacturing and industry

Manufacturing. Broadly speaking, manufacturing ranges from under 20% of GDP in America to about 30% in Germany and Japan (see Table 9.1). Manufacturing is tiny in some African states, but it rises to 35–40% of GDP in developing countries such as Macau, Puerto Rico and Taiwan.

Table 9.2 shows the relative importance of various manufacturing sectors across *The Economist 13*.

Industry. The difference between manufacturing and industrial production accounts for about 10% of GDP on average. This takes total industrial production to 30% of American GDP and 40% of Japan's (see Table 9.1).

The gap between manufacturing and industrial production is more significant where the energy producing sector is large, but even OPEC members' industrial production rarely exceeds about half of GDP.

Interpretation

Industrial production as a whole is broadly indicative of the state of the economic cycle. The output of industries producing capital goods and consumer durables tend to be squeezed most during a

Figure 9.2

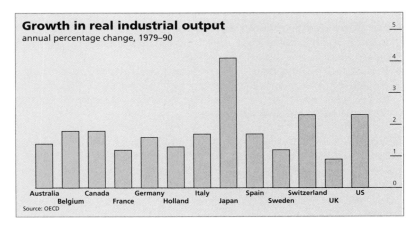

Growth in real industrial output
annual percentage change, 1979–90

Australia Canada Germany Italy Spain Switzerland US
Belgium France Holland Japan Sweden UK
Source: OECD

downturn. Some countries produce separate figures for various sectors (see Motor vehicles, page 111). Steel production is a useful lead indicator since it is an input to many other industries.

Table 9.2 **Structure of manufacturing, % shares, 1990[a]**

	Food, beverages & tobacco	Textiles & clothing	Machinery & transport equipment	Chemicals	Other
Australia	18	8	19	8	46
Belgium	20	8	23	14	36
Canada	14	6	26	9	46
France	13	7	30	9	42
Germany	9	4	41	13	32
Holland	19	3	25	14	38
Italy	8	13	32	10	36
Japan	9	5	38	10	38
Spain	19	8	24	10	39
Sweden	10	2	34	9	46
Switzerland	10	7	31	9	42
UK	13	6	32	12	38
USA	12	5	35	10	38

Source: World Bank

CAPACITY USE AND UTILISATION

Measures: Extent to which plant and machinery is in use.
Significance: Indicator of output and inflationary pressures.
Presented as: Percentage of total capacity.
Focus on: Absolute level and trends.
Yardstick: 80–90%; more may be inflationary, less indicates room for growth.
Released: Monthly, 1–3 months in arrears; revised.

Overview

Total capacity. Capacity is a vague, hard to measure concept which varies over time and according to economic conditions. The term is generally used to refer to the sustainable maximum output that could be produced by existing (installed) manufacturing plant and machinery, although sometimes other factors such as labour are taken into account. Either way "normal capacity" will vary if working practices are changed, even if only by increasing the working week by one hour. (See Productivity, page 49).

Capacity use. Capacity use is usually defined as output divided by sustainable maximum capacity. Sustainable maximum output is lower than temporarily attainable peak production, so use of (sustainable) capacity can and occasionally does exceed 100% in some industries.

Overall capacity use does not go as high as 100% because different companies reach their peaks at different stages of the economic cycle. Also bottlenecks in one industry restrict supplies and therefore output in another: in major cyclical peaks, a shortage of metals can limit output of consumer durables and business machinery, and restrain capacity utilisation in those industries.

Capital investment. Figures for capital investment are sometimes taken as indicators of changes in capacity, but investment is usually measured gross, with no allowance for scrapping. Even where allowance is made, the net capital stock may not be representative of output potential. Moreover the increase in capacity derived from a unit of new capital is affected by factors such as new technology, an increasingly shorter life for capital equipment, a longer work week for capital, restructuring of industry and the closure of plants.

Interpretation

Strong economic growth with high capacity use suggests inflationary pressures. However, if demand is expected to remain buoyant and if interest rates are low, producers may invest in new plant and machinery.

If the economy is expanding, but there is low capacity use and no evidence of recent new investment, it may be that the economy is recovering from recession.

American capacity utilisation

The US Federal Reserve is one of the few national official bodies to produce estimates of capacity use and its figures are undoubtedly the most detailed and consistent available, but not even the Fed conducts surveys of capacity or capacity utilisation. Instead it uses data from the Bureau of the Census and various trade organisations to estimate capacity in various industries. Overall capacity utilisation is industrial production divided by the capacity index.

The Fed defines capacity as the realistically sustainable maximum capacity, rather than unsustainable short-term peak capacity.

American capacity use exceeded 90% during the Korean and Vietnam wars, but it has been below 90% since 1967. A figure of 88% overall would indicate severe strains (but 88% would be normal in certain individual industries which operate a high level of capacity use, such as paper and pulp).

Surveys

In most other countries measures of capacity use are derived from survey evidence (see Business conditions, page 103). For example, the CBI's monthly survey asks British manufacturers if their capacity is satisfactory in relation to orders. Defining "capacity" and "satisfactory" is left to respondents. About half include factors other than physical capacity and the interpretation of satisfactory has changed over time.

Accordingly, survey results are better for examining short-term rather than long-term changes in capacity use.

MANUFACTURING ORDERS

Measures: New orders received by manufacturing companies.
Significance: Indicator of output in the near term.
Presented as: Money, index or percentage balance form.
Focus on: Trends.
Yardstick: Total orders can change by 10–20%. Generally the higher the better, but watch for bottlenecks and inflation.
Released: Monthly, 1–2 months in arrears; revised.

Overview

- **The US Commerce Department** publishes new orders received by manufacturing companies and their unfilled orders in current dollars, with a breakdown between orders for durables and non-durable goods.
- **The German Federal Statistical Office** publishes volume index numbers for manufacturing orders, distinguishing between domestic and foreign orders.
- **The Confederation of British Industry** publishes survey results indicating the percentage of respondent companies which think that order books are satisfactory less the percentage of companies reporting unsatisfactory order books. This subjective assessment of total and export orders is broken down into value and volume terms.

Manufacturing orders (including machine tool orders) ripple through the economy. An order for a washing machine may prompt an order for a metal pressing which in turn will provoke an order for sheet steel. Each order will reflect the output price, while manufacturing output and GDP will rise by the value-added component only. Orders are therefore much more volatile than manufacturing production.

Total orders

Buoyant order books indicate upward pressure on employment and output over the next few months. This is basically good, but it may suggest a rise in inflation if unemployment is low; capacity use is high; there is an order backlog (orders are high in relation to shipments or sales); and/or inventories are low. Strong orders will also tend to increase imports of materials and intermediate goods, but this may be offset by exports (see below).

Orders provide an early signal of changes in the economic cycle. A rise in orders may indicate the end of a recession; a fall may indicate that the cycle is peaking.

Where orders are presented in value terms they should be adjusted for inflation. Producer prices can be used. If orders rise by 6% in value and producer prices increase by 4%, the volume of orders is about 2% higher. It is important to ascertain that this adjustment does not reflect, say, a movement in refined oil prices which are erratic and can falsely suggest changes in the volume of new orders. There may also be other blips. In the American series the transport component jumps by perhaps 40% in a month when new aircraft are ordered. Try to use a series which excludes misleading influences.

Domestic orders

Domestic orders by sector are indicative of the structure of home demand. Bigger orders for capital goods suggest more investment activity and more output in the future. Machine tool orders sometimes receive special attention: an increase is encouraging because they are used to manufacture yet more machines which in turn make more goods.

Defence orders tend to reflect political decision-making. If they are identified separately, as they are in America, subtract them from capital or durable orders to get a better feel for underlying demand.

Orders for durable and capital goods react to changes in the economic cycle ahead of other orders. Orders for consumer goods are obviously indicative of trends in the consumer sector.

Export orders

Orders from overseas reflect export competitiveness (see page 154) and the economic cycle in overseas markets. A rise is good, but see comments above about inflation. If orders are booked despite a stronger currency, profits may be squeezed and repeat business may not be sustained.

MOTOR VEHICLES

Measures: Activity involving cars and trucks.
Significance: Indicator of manufacturing production as well as consumer demand.
Presented as: Number of units.
Focus on: Trends.
Yardstick: Volatile, but a 12-month change of more than a few percentage points is worrying.
Released: Monthly; more frequently in America.

Overview

There are three main series relating to motor vehicles:

• manufacturers' production;
• sales; and
• registrations of new vehicles with national licensing authorities.

Registrations and sales are broadly similar; the difference mainly reflects the method of data collection.

The figures usually relate to the number of units, that is, volume rather than value. They may not reveal very much about the pattern of demand for cheap or expensive vehicles or about changes in quality. However, they are a useful indicator of manufacturing production; demand for a durable good which is very vulnerable to the economic cycle; competitive pressures, especially between domestic and overseas producers; and import and export trends.

Interpretation

Vehicle sales are a reasonable leading indicator of economic activity. A vehicle purchased by an individual is classed as consumption expenditure. The same vehicle purchased by a business is investment spending. Generally, then, figures for cars are suggestive of consumption; light vans and trucks are indicative of investment.

111

Production and sales may not tally due to changes in stocks (see Wholesale stocks and Retail stocks, pages 116 and 117) and net exports.

Seasonality. There is a marked seasonal pattern in car sales, with turnover bunched into January and, if different, the start of a new model year or registration plate year identifier. Discounting price wars can also shift demand into a different month from normal. Short-term figures should be interpreted with care. Take 2–3 months together and compare with similar periods of earlier years.

Table 9.3 **Motor vehicle markets**
'000 per month

	Production		Registrations	
	1989	1990	1989	1990
Australia	na	na	39	41
Belgium	na	na	39	42
Canada	82	78	82	74
France[a]	306	292	190	192
Germany[b]	343	347	236	255
Holland	na	na	41	42
Italy	164	156	168	203
Japan	754	829	370	430
Spain	141	145	96	84
Sweden	na	na	26	20
Switzerland	na	na	26	27
UK	108	108	192	167
USA	569	504	989	946
EC	1062	1047	988	1012
OECD	na	na	2574	2603

[a] Figures are distorted because registrations for December 1989 were processed in January 1990 because of strikes in police stations.
[b] Sales were strong in 1990 due to the opening of the market in eastern Germany.

Source: OECD

CONSTRUCTION ORDERS AND OUTPUT

Measures: Activity in the construction sector.
Significance: Indicator of new investment and future output.
Presented as: Value of orders, volume of construction.
Focus on: Trends in volume terms.
Yardstick: OECD average non-residential construction volume rose by 1.8% a year during the 1980s.
Released: Monthly, at least one month in arrears.

Overview

There are several main series, including the following.

- Orders (volume in Britain; value in Japan and America).
- Permits issued (number in Belgium and France; value in Australia, Canada, Germany, Holland).
- The value of work put in place (Germany, America).
- Value-added in money and real terms (with GDP figures for expenditure on investment for many countries).

Construction covers buildings and infrastructure (such as roads and ports). Orders are sometimes based on contracting work. This may include projects such as oil rigs which really belong in manufacturing production under steel fabrication. The figures usually exclude residential dwellings, but this should be checked.

Significance

Construction work is fixed investment. This boosts current period GDP and lays the basis for future economic growth. Its share of GDP in different countries is shown in Table 8.2.

New factories and offices provide a direct foundation for higher economic output. New infrastructure improves social welfare and generally boosts productivity. The only real exception to the "future output" rule is investment in new dwellings, but this still brings benefits (see Housing, page 114).

Interpretation

Seasons and cycles. Construction work is highly seasonal and cyclical. Data are frequently (but not always) seasonally adjusted, but it is wise to take 2–3 months together and compare them with the same periods in earlier years. It is important to look out for the adverse effects of a wet or freezing month.

Construction activity is sensitive to expectations of future demand and to interest rates. Low interest rates increase the return from investment and encourage capital spending, especially when they are coupled with strong demand and high usage of existing capacity. (See also Investment, page 90.)

Orders. Construction orders signal demand for building materials and labour over the coming months (and years – depending on the size of the individual projects). Knock-on effects include implications for service industries such as architects and surveyors, manufacturers of industrial plant to go into new factories, and

113

providers of office fittings and furnishings.

Orders are often given on a value basis. These should be adjusted for inflation to arrive at the volume change. For example, if the value of orders rises by 10% and inflation is 8%, real growth is about 2%. Producer prices might be used for deflation if there is no obviously better indicator to hand. Figures sometimes cover construction permits; these provide no guide to the size of the projects, and they may not be translated into construction activity if economic conditions change.

Output. Construction output in volume terms helps you to judge the effect on total output. Construction accounts for about 5% of GDP, so a 10% rise in construction value-added contributes around 0.5% to GDP.

A large construction project spread over several months or years adds a little bit to output in each of several periods. (See above for knock-on effects.)

HOUSING STARTS, COMPLETIONS AND SALES

Measures: Number of new houses begun and finished; sales of new and existing homes.

Significance: Indicator of construction activity; industrial and consumer demand.

Presented as: Number of units per month.

Focus on: Trends.

Yardstick: Volatile; number of starts can change by 40% a year. OECD residential construction volume increased by 1.1% a year during the 1980s.

Released: Monthly, at least one month in arrears.

Overview

There are three main series indicating:

- the number of residential dwellings started;
- the number of residential dwellings completed; and
- the number of residential dwellings sold.

Each series applies to a given period, usually one month. They are often seasonally adjusted, but it is wise to take 2–3 months together and compare with the same periods in earlier years since house building is highly sensitive to the weather.

Figures usually distinguish between public and private dwellings. Activity in the private sector is a good guide to underlying activity, but there are also knock-on effects from public sector building.

Starts

A housing start is counted on the date that foundations are begun (not when the site is cleared). It implies a given level of demand for construction materials and labour over the next few months and a housing completion at the end of that period.

If the existing housing stock is old, there may be an element of replacement building. Generally, however, housing starts (and completions) are closely linked to population growth rates, earnings and employment, and interest rates.

Completions

A housing completion implies a house sale, a new mortgage advance and increased consumer demand for carpets, furnishings and other durables – possibly accompanied by extra consumer credit.

Sales

Housing sales are linked to the level of completions, but turnover of existing homes is more important. House prices are highly relevant. People are more inclined to move home and buy rather than rent when house prices are rising and are expected to provide capital gains. Housing turnover is also stimulated by incomes rising relative to house prices and by lower mortgage rates which encourage borrowing.

Effect on GDP

The construction of new houses is classed as fixed investment in residential dwellings. This accounts for only a few percentage points of GDP (see Table 8.2), so arithmetically a 10% rise in house building may add less than 0.5% to total output.

The sale of existing houses is a transfer of production scored in earlier periods and does not itself add to output, but real estate, legal and financial fees and commissions do, as does demand for new furnishing and other durables.

HOUSING

A good leading indicator of economic activity is residential construction. As interest rates rise, housing starts fall, indicating a downturn; a revival of house-building usually

115

signals a recovery. Japan's slowdown was introduced by a fall in housing starts in the second half of last year; starts in January 1992 were down by a quarter from the peak of July–September 1990. In America starts rose steadily during 1991, boosting hopes of economic recovery. Housing starts are less clear about Britain's prospects: the rise that began last summer was quickly interrupted. In the third quarter of 1991 house-building in western Germany was booming, belying the economic slowdown; starts were up 10% over the previous quarter.

The Economist, March 28th 1992

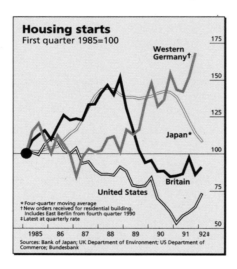

WHOLESALE SALES OR TURNOVER, ORDERS AND STOCKS

Measures:	Most common indicator measures sales by wholesalers.
Significance:	Indicator of demand.
Presented as:	Monthly index numbers.
Focus on:	Rates of change in volume of sales.
Yardstick:	More volatile than retail sales; look for gains of 3–4% a year.
Released:	Monthly, 1–2 months in arrears; revised.

Overview

Wholesale sales (called wholesale turnover in Germany) are an important link in the supply chain. Wholesalers channel imports and domestically produced or processed goods through to final

116

users. Where stocks and orders are available, these provide a useful check on trends. A fall in wholesale sales or a rise in wholesale inventories suggests or confirms slack in business and retail demand.

There are relatively few figures on the service sector, but wholesale sales provide extremely loose indicators of demand from, for example, hotels and catering establishments. They are also indicative of demand for business goods including, in some countries, building materials. Wholesale sales are a reasonable signal of consumer demand (but retail sales are better – see below).

Value and volume

It is important to watch the volume of sales, particularly for durable goods (an early indicator of demand pressures). Where figures are in value terms they can be converted to volume using wholesale or producer prices. For example, if producer prices increase by 3% and sales value rises by 5%, volume is up by about 2%.

Effect on GDP

Wholesale sales are included in the distributive trades sector of GDP. Their direct contribution is wholesalers' value added (income from sales less the cost of purchases and other inputs).

RETAIL SALES OR TURNOVER, ORDERS AND STOCKS

Measures: Most commonly sales by retailers.
Significance: Indicator of consumer demand.
Presented as: Monthly index numbers.
Focus on: Rates of change in volume of sales.
Yardstick: 3% a year is reasonable; any lower and the economy might slow down. More than 4–5% suggests overheating.
Released: Monthly, at least one month in arrears.

Coverage

Retail sales figures provide an important and timely indicator of spending at retail outlets. The series is known as retail turnover in Germany; department store sales (with more limited coverage) in Italy and Japan; and hypermarket sales in Spain. French figures cover only department and chain stores, mail order firms and hypermarkets. Sweden's series excludes alcohol, pharmaceuticals,

117

cars and petrol.

Most series include VAT or sales taxes and many are in volume terms, but the Dutch, Japanese, Italian, Spanish, Swedish and Swiss indices are in value terms only (that is, before adjustment for inflation).

Headline series in North America are also in value terms, but in dollars. Canadian retail sales figures included federal sales tax up to January 1991 but have since excluded the goods and services tax. Australia produces a monthly value and a quarterly volume index; both in dollars.

Basis. Information is presented by type of business, rather than by commodity. For example, food sales appear under at least two sub-headings: food retailers and mixed businesses. Where an establishment sells items outside its main classification, such as sales of food by a petrol filling station, these are usually excluded from the statistics. Credit sales are treated as a sale, valued at the date of the transaction at the total credit price including charges levied by the retailer.

Interpretation

Retail sales cover up to half of total consumer spending although there is not a direct correlation between the two since some items sold by retailers are bought by businesses. Nevertheless, retail sales are a key indicator of consumer confidence and demand.

It is important to focus on volume increases. Where figures are in value terms they can be converted to volume using consumer prices. Arithmetically, a 1% rise in retail sales adds roughly 0.3% to GDP, all else being constant.

Seasonality. Retail sales data are usually seasonally adjusted, but they should be interpreted with care. Promotional sales price discounting, warm weather or an expectation of increases in sales taxes can encourage consumers to bring forward their spending. An upward blip may not be sustained.

Cyclical variations. In times of financial stress consumers cut back on non-essential spending, which results in a decline or less rapid growth in retail sales. Spending on durables (items with a life of over one year, such as washing machines) goes first. For example, in Britain during the 1982 recession, the volume of food sales fell by a mere 5% while the volume of turnover at retailers of household goods slumped by 15%.

Although retail sales are very nearly coincident with GDP, retail sales figures are published with a much shorter lag. They therefore provide an early indication of economic trends.

A downturn in retail sales could lead to lower wholesale sales, slacker factory orders, an accumulation of stocks and, eventually, a cutback in production.

Stocks and orders. Where figures for retail stocks and orders are also available they provide useful advance warning. For example, excess retail demand might show up first in a fall in the ratio of retailers' inventories to sales. This spells trouble if wholesalers' and manufacturers' stocks are also low and there are constraints on manufacturers' ability to increase output (high capacity use and low unemployment). Look out for price inflation and a surge in imports.

10

THE BALANCE OF PAYMENTS

"No nation was ever ruined by trade."
Benjamin Franklin

The balance of payments is a continual source of misunderstanding and misconception. Yet it is no more than a simple accounting record of international flows. Moreover, trade between two countries is exactly the same as trade between two individuals. Once seen in this light, interpreting external flows is no different from interpreting any other economic transactions.

ACCOUNTING CONVENTIONS

Balance of payments accounts record financial flows in a specific period such as one year. Financial inflows (such as receipts for exports or when a foreigner invests in the stockmarket) are treated as credits or positive entries. Outflows (such as payments for imports or the purchase of shares on a foreign stockmarket) are debits or negative entries. When a foreigner invests in (acquires a claim on) the country, there is a capital inflow which is a credit entry. Conversely, the acquisition of a claim on another country is a negative or debit entry.

Debits = credits. The accounts are double entry, that is, every transaction is entered twice. For example, the export of goods involves the receipt of cash (the credit) which represents a claim on another country (the debit). By definition the balance of payments must balance. Debits must equal credits.

Current = capital. One side of each transaction is treated as a current flow (such as a receipt of payment for an export). The other is a capital flow (such as the acquisition of a claim on another country). Arithmetically current flows must exactly equal capital flows.

Balances

The accounts build up in layers. Balances may be struck at each stage.

Net exports of goods (exports of goods less imports of goods)
  = the visible trade or merchandise trade balance
  + net exports of services (such as shipping and insurance)
  = the balance of trade in goods and services
  + net rent, interest, profits and dividends (RIPDs)
  + net current transfers (such as payments of international aid and workers' remittances)
  = the current-account balance (all the following entries form the capital account)
  + net direct investment (such as building a factory overseas)
  = the core balance
  + other net long-term capital movements (such as portfolio investments in foreign equity markets)
  = the basic balance
  + net short-term capital movements (including bank deposits and speculative buying of an appreciating currency for a quick profit)
  = the balance of total currency flows (or the balance for official financing)
  + net official financing, sometimes known as accommodating items (government capital movements such as changes in balances at the IMF or changes in official currency reserves)
  = zero

Thus the current account covers trade in goods and services, RIPDs and transfers. Non-merchandise items are known as invisibles. All other flows are recorded in the capital account.

Official financing exactly balances "total currency flows", filling the gap between market supply and demand for a currency.

Balancing items

In practice it is impossible to identify all flows: invisibles are hard to track, some speculative flows go unmeasured and some transactions are concealed by tax evasion or organised crime. Even visible trade is sometimes overlooked. In the late 1980s British customs officials stumbled upon £1.5 billion of aircraft imports which had previously gone unnoticed. In addition, the balance of payments accounts relate to specific periods such as calendar years. Lags mean that one-half of a transaction may not be recorded in the same period as the other half.

To cover timing differences and unidentified items, government statisticians are forced to make the accounts balance with a residual or balancing item.

Interpretation. Every country has discrepancies and Britain's are among the worst. In 1989 the accounts showed a current-account deficit of £19 billion with a capital-account surplus of £4 billion, leaving a massive £15 billion unidentified balancing item. (After a special search this was partly reallocated, mostly in the capital account.)

Aggregating international trade figures implies that world imports exceed world exports by up to $100 billion a year. Apart from being absurd, this makes it very difficult to interpret balance of payments data. What it means is that many countries have smaller current-account deficits or larger surpluses than they think, or even surpluses rather than deficits.

Deficits and surpluses

The balance of payments must balance. When commentators talk about a balance of payments deficit or surplus, they mean a deficit or surplus on one part of the accounts.

Attention once focused on the current-account balance, but capital flows have become increasingly important as many industrial countries relaxed exchange controls and other barriers to world capital flows during the 1980s. Capital flows grew by 20% a year in 1983–88, four times the rate of growth in trade.

The balance to watch. The best way to define a deficit or surplus is as an imbalance between supply and demand for the currency. The figure for "total currency flows" in the balance of payments accounts is indicative of overall market pressures on the exchange rate. However, since the total includes speculative flows, the basic balance (the current-account balance plus net long-term capital flows) is probably a better indicator of underlying supply and demand pressures. Indeed, it might be argued that since investment in equities and bonds is nearly as volatile as short-term capital, the core balance (the basic balance excluding portfolio investment) is better still as an indicator of underlying pressures.

Balance of payments accounting quirks

Balance of payments figures must be interpreted with care. As a brief illustration, consider a company which borrows $500 in foreign currency from a domestic bank (which itself borrows the cash from overseas) and invests the money in an overseas operation

which earns profits of $1,750, only $750 of which are repatriated.
If the balance of payments accounts are drawn up in accordance with IMF recommendations and if all transactions are identified, the entries will be as follows.

	$
Current account	
Rent, interest, profits and	
dividends: profits earned abroad	1,750
Capital account	
Private investment overseas	−1,500
of which:	
Financed by borrowing	−500
Unremitted profits	−1,000
Banks' overseas borrowing	+500
Change in reserves (− = additions)	−750

At first glance the accounts suggest that there was an investment outflow of $1,500. Yet the net currency movement is the inflow of $750 profits.

Analysis of balance of payments accounts requires careful review of all entries and a good measure of imagination. Do not be misled by changes in reserves, where negative entries indicate an increase in official holdings of foreign currencies.

Published figures

National accounting practices vary, but in general governments produce two sets of figures relating to external flows.

- Overseas trade statistics (OTS), which measure imports and exports of goods and services.
- Balance of payments (BOP) accounts, which record all cross-border currency flows including movements of capital, with emphasis on transactions rather than physical movement.

Apart from the fact that balance of payments accounts have a wider coverage, the main difference is that BOP accounts exclude goods passing across borders where there is no change of ownership, but include changes of ownership which take place abroad (such as ships built and delivered abroad).

In addition, overseas trade statistics usually record the value of trade at the point of customs clearance, measuring exports FOB (free on board) and imports CIF (including cost, insurance and freight). For BOP purposes insurance and freight are separated out and imports of goods are shown FOB. Transport and insurance are

123

shown as imports of services if the payments are made to overseas companies; otherwise they are domestic transactions which are excluded from the accounts.

Using OTS figures. Figures on an OTS basis are usually the first available and they are preferable for examining the effect of imports on domestic economic activity. They usually show imports cif which is the cost at the point of arrival and is directly comparable with the cost of goods produced at home.

Using BOP figures. BOP figures should be used for analysis of external trade in relation to GDP. Exports and imports of goods and services on a BOP basis match the figures in GDP. The total of rents, interest, profits and dividends plus net current transfers is shown as "net income from abroad" in national accounts statistics (the difference between GDP and GNP).

Other figures. The briefs in this section should be read in conjunction with the exchange-rate briefs (Chapter 11).

Imports and export unit values (prices) are included with other price indicators in Chapter 10 (page 194).

IMPORTS OF GOODS AND SERVICES

Measures: Purchases from abroad.
Significance Imports add to well-being but may displace domestic production and drain financial resources.
Presented as: Value and volume figures in money and index form.
Focus on: Growth; total in relation to exports (see trade balance) and as a percentage of GDP.
Yardstick: OECD average growth in the volume of imports of goods and services was 4.9% a year during the 1980s.
Released: Monthly, at least one month in arrears.

Overview

A country imports goods and services because it cannot produce them itself or because there is comparative advantage in buying them from abroad. Some commentators worry that all imports are a drain on national resources, which is a bit like saying you should not buy from a domestic neighbour who produces something better or cheaper than you do. Of course, you can only buy to the extent that you can finance the purchase from income, savings or borrowing against future production.

Figure 10.1

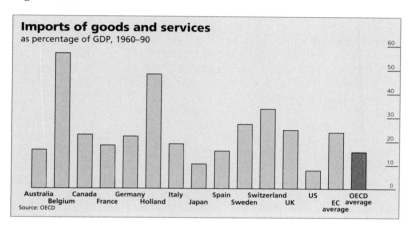

Imports of goods and services
as percentage of GDP, 1960–90

Australia Canada Germany Italy Spain Switzerland US OECD
Belgium France Holland Japan Sweden UK EC average
Source: OECD average

Goods and services. Merchandise or visible imports relate to physical goods. Imports of services are payments to foreigners for invisibles such as shipping, travel and tourism; financial services including insurance, banking, commodity trading and brokerage; and other items such as advertising, education, health, commissions and royalties.

In practice, many countries give prominence to visible trade figures because they are among the most reliable and rapidly available figures on external flows. Even so, they are available only after a lag, are frequently revised as more information comes to hand and are subject to various errors and omissions. Figures for invisibles are harder to collect, less reliable and are published only quarterly by some countries.

Value and volume. Changes in import values reflect changes in foreign prices, exchange rates and quantity (volume). Real exchange rates (see page 154) are useful for identifying price and currency effects. Import volume indicates "real changes", and value gives the overall balance of payments position.

Cyclical variation. Import volumes tend to move cyclically. In general they increase when home demand is buoyant. For this reason imports might be seen as a safety valve which offsets the inflationary pressures that arise when domestic firms are operating at close to full capacity.

Link to exports. Imports are also linked to exports. An increase in exports boosts GDP because the goods sold overseas are part of domestic production.

125

When GDP increases, demand for domestic and imported goods rises as well.

Import penetration. Imports of goods and services as a percentage of GDP (or of total final demand) indicates the degree of dependence on imports; the higher the figure the more imports displace domestic output and the more vulnerable is the economy to changes in import prices. A sudden rise in import penetration may signal that domestic companies are operating at full capacity and cannot meet increases in demand.

Import composition and sources

Commodity breakdown. A high volume of imports of intermediate and capital goods is generally good where these are used to manufacture other items or to generate invisible earnings. This adds value to GDP and perhaps contributes to future export growth. For example, a country buying aircraft from abroad records these as imports. In later years the aircraft will be used to move passengers and generate profits which are invisible export earnings.

Note though that manufacturing output declines in the short term when imports displace locally processed or manufactured items. Developing countries increasingly export semi-manufactures (such as cloth and refined petroleum products) rather than raw materials (such as cotton and crude oil) and the industrial countries import more semi-manufactures and fewer raw materials.

Increases in the volume of imports of consumer goods are a direct signal of consumer demand. They imply that domestic producers cannot meet the required price, quality or quantity.

Compressibility. When examining a developing country it is important to check the compressibility of imports, that is, the extent to which there are non-essential goods which need not be imported in times of stress on the balance of payments. If all imports are essentials such as foods and fuels it may not be possible to reduce the import bill.

Sources. A country which imports from just one or two main trading partners is vulnerable to economic shocks from its suppliers, especially if they cease to export those particular goods, if prices rise sharply or if there is some political disturbance.

International comparisons

The distinction between OTS and BOP figures is discussed on

Table 10.1   **Imports of goods and services**

	% of GDP 1960–90	Real annual % change				
		1960–68	1968–73	1973–79	1979–89	1990
Australia	16.2	6.3	3.3	3.7	6.7	−3.3
Belgium	56.5	7.8	10.8	3.8	3.3	4.6
Canada	22.6	7.4	9.2	6.0	6.2	0.8
France	18.1	9.5	11.9	3.6	3.7	6.4
Germany	21.8	7.6	10.3	5.2	3.1	11.9
Holland	48.0	8.7	10.1	3.3	3.1	4.4
Italy	18.8	9.7	11.2	3.1	4.4	6.7
Japan	10.5	13.6	15.1	3.5	4.8	11.7
Spain	15.9	20.2	12.6	3.4	7.3	8.1
Sweden	27.1	6.1	6.0	2.7	3.5	0.5
Switzerland	33.5	7.3	9.3	3.5	4.3	3.5
UK	24.7	4.1	6.8	2.1	5.1	1.6
USA	7.7	7.4	7.9	3.5	6.0	2.8
EC	23.7	8.0	10.1	3.5	4.2	7.0
OECD	15.6	7.9	9.8	3.5	4.9	5.9

Source: OECD

pages 123–124. For international comparisons, aim for consistency and watch the FOB/CIF basis. As a crude rule of thumb, imports CIF are around 12% greater than imports FOB. The figure varies from 20% for Latin American countries, such as Bolivia, to under 4% for North America and some European countries, such as Germany, where local cross-border trade keeps shipping costs lower than for geographically remote countries.

Other special factors

Smoothing. Various special factors can cause swings in trade figures even when there is no change in underlying trends. It is always wise to take at least 2–3 months together to smooth out blips.

Many commentators compare the calendar year so far with the same period of the previous year. This has a certain neatness, but economic figures do not respect accounting periods and comparisons of, say, the two months to February are more susceptible to erratic influences than the 11 months to November.

Oil and erratics. The movement of high value items such as ships, aircraft and precious stones can have a significant effect on trade figures. Oil accounts for a large proportion of imports for many countries (typically up to 25%) and the price can fluctuate widely. For these reasons many countries publish figures for imports and exports excluding oil and erratics, which helps to identify underlying trends.

Figure 10.2

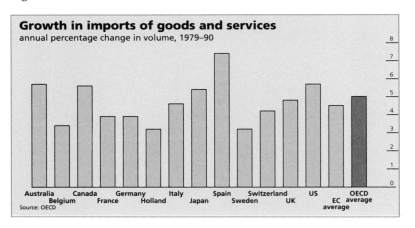

Growth in imports of goods and services
annual percentage change in volume, 1979–90

Australia   Canada   Germany   Italy   Spain   Switzerland   US   OECD
Belgium   France   Holland   Japan   Sweden   UK   EC   average
Source: OECD   average

Seasonal adjustment. Most trade figures are adjusted for obvious seasonal factors such as climatic variation and the effect of holidays on industrial output. However, seasonal adjustment cannot cope with shipping and dock strikes, unusually bad weather or the movement of high value items. Sensible adjustments should be made for any such factors of which you are aware.

EXPORTS OF GOODS AND SERVICES

Measures: Sales in other countries.
Significance: Exports generate foreign currency and economic growth.
Presented as: Value and volume figures in money and index numbers.
Focus on: Growth; total in relation to imports (see trade balance) and as a percentage of GDP.
Yardstick: OECD average growth in the volume of exports of goods and services was 5.0% a year during the 1980s.
Released: Monthly, at least one month in arrears.

Overview

Exports generate foreign currency earnings. Export growth boosts GDP which in turn implies more imports, so exports should never be considered in isolation.

This brief should be read in conjunction with the previous brief on imports. Note especially the comments on goods and services (page 125) and special factors (page 127).

Table 10.2   **Exports of goods and services**

	% of GDP 1960–90	Annual real % change				
		1960–68	1968–73	1973–79	1979–89	1990
Australia	15.4	7.1	8.0	4.6	4.4	11.6
Belgium	57.3	8.4	11.0	3.1	4.2	5.0
Canada	23.5	9.3	8.0	4.6	5.1	3.8
France	18.3	6.9	12.9	6.4	3.6	5.2
Germany	24.4	7.7	7.8	4.3	4.5	9.9
Holland	49.7	7.2	11.9	2.9	3.9	4.7
Italy	18.8	11.8	7.6	7.9	2.9	7.5
Japan	11.6	15.1	12.7	8.9	7.5	10.9
Spain	14.6	10.4	14.1	5.2	5.7	4.2
Sweden	27.4	7.0	8.8	2.5	3.7	1.2
Switzerland	33.2	6.5	7.6	3.1	3.5	3.0
UK	24.2	4.1	6.8	4.0	2.9	4.8
USA	7.1	4.9	9.4	5.0	6.4	6.4
EC	23.9	7.3	9.2	4.8	4.0	6.7
OECD	15.5	7.2	9.3	5.0	5.0	7.3

Source: OECD

Value and volume. Demand for exports depends on economic conditions in foreign countries, prices (relative inflation and the exchange rate) and perceptions of quality, reliability, and so on. Real exchange rates (see page 154) help to identify inflation and currency effects. Export volume indicates "real changes", and value gives the overall balance of payments position.

Composition and destinations. As with imports, dependence on a few commodities increases vulnerability to shifts in demand

Figure 10.3

129

Figure 10.4

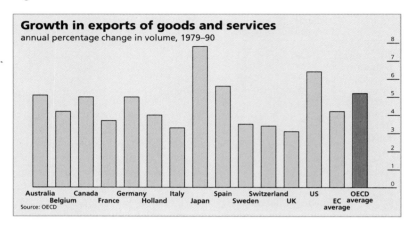

while dependence on a few countries increases vulnerability to their economic cycle.

The greater the proportion of exports in relation to GDP, the bigger the boost to domestic output when overseas demand rises. For example, Holland's exports account for nearly 60% of GDP and it trades heavily with Germany. Consequently, if German imports rise by 10%, Dutch GDP jumps by 1.5%. A high exports/GDP ratio also implies a larger slump when foreign demand falls.

Compatibility

Exports are always measured FOB (free on board) or FAS (free alongside ship) at the point of export, so they present fewer compatibility problems than imports which may be FOB or may include insurance and freight (CIF).

TRADE BALANCE, MERCHANDISE TRADE BALANCE

Measures: The net balance between exports and imports of goods.
Significance: Shows a country's fundamental trading position.
Presented as: Money values.
Focus on: Total balance; balance in relation to the current account.
Yardstick: A deficit is potentially more of a problem than a surplus. See Current-account yardstick (page 133).
Released: Monthly, at least one month in arrears.

Overview

The trade balance is the difference between exports and imports (see above). It may measure visible (merchandise) trade only, or trade in both goods and services.

Invisibles are difficult to measure, so the balance of trade in goods and services is less reliable and more likely to be revised than the visible balance.

This brief should be read in conjunction with the previous briefs on exports and imports. Note especially the comments on goods and services (page 125) and special factors (page 127).

Arithmetic. Small variations in imports or exports can have a significant effect on the trade balance. For example, if exports are $10 billion and imports are $11 billion, a 10% rise in imports to $12 billion will double the trade deficit from $1 billion to $2 billion.

Income elasticity. The relationship of exports and imports to economic growth (their income elasticity) is important. For example, Japan's imports tend to increase by a relatively small amount when its GDP grows by 1%. At the same time its exports rise rapidly when its trading partners' economies expand. Thus, if Japan's economy grows at the same pace as the rest of the world, its trade surplus will tend to widen.

Supply constraints. A large trade deficit may signal supply constraints, especially if it is accompanied by high inflation and/or the deficit has emerged recently due to a rise in imports. This suggests that companies are unable to boost output to match higher domestic demand. The deficit may act as a safety valve and divert potentially inflationary pressures. Alternatively, an increasing trade deficit may signal a loss of competitiveness by domestic companies.

Net savings and the resource gap. The balance of trade in goods and services measures the relationship between national savings and investment. A deficit indicates that investment exceeds savings and that absorption of real resources exceeds output.

For developing countries, the difference between exports and imports of goods and services is more usually called the resource gap; that is, the extent to which the country is dependent on the outside world. In the 1980s and early 1990s many developing countries had a resource gap equivalent to 20–30% of GDP. Lesotho's was around 100%.

131

Table 10.3   **Trade and current-account balances**
% of GDP (except final column)

	Net exports of goods & services	Current-account balance					$bn
	1960–90	1960–68	1968–73	1973–79	1979–89	1990	1990
Australia	−0.9	−2.3	−1.0	−2.0	−4.6	−4.8	−14.3
Belgium	0.8	0.2	2.1	−0.8	−0.7	1.8	3.6
Canada	0.9	−1.7	−0.2	−2.2	−1.3	−3.3	−18.9
France	0.3	1.2	0.5	0.2	−0.4	−1.1	−13.6
Germany	2.6	0.5	1.1	1.0	2.0	3.2	47.9
Holland	1.7	0.5	0.9	1.2	2.5	3.7	10.3
Italy	nil	1.0	1.0	−0.1	−0.9	−1.3	−14.4
Japan	1.1	nil	1.3	0.3	2.1	1.2	35.4
Spain	−1.3	nil	0.4	−1.5	−0.8	−3.4	−16.9
Sweden	0.3	−0.1	0.5	−1.4	−1.7	−2.6	−5.8
Switzerland	−0.3	−1.1	1.4	4.2	3.9	3.8	8.6
UK	−0.5	−0.3	0.2	−1.2	−0.6	−2.5	−24.5
USA	−0.6	0.7	0.2	0.3	−1.7	−1.7	−92.3
EC	0.2	0.3	0.6	−0.3	−0.1	−0.1	−8.2
OECD	−0.1	0.3	0.5	−0.2	−0.6	−0.6	−101.6

Source: OECD

Current flows. For the industrial countries a trade imbalance is not necessarily a problem; it reflects choice as much as necessity.

For most of the past 200 years Britain has run a deficit on visible trade which has been more than offset by one of the world's largest surpluses on invisibles. Meanwhile countries with large manufacturing sectors, such as Japan and Germany, have tended to run visible-trade surpluses and invisibles deficits. The current account is a better indicator of overall current flows (see page 133).

Eliminating a trade deficit

There are two main ways in which an external trade deficit might move back into balance.

- **A change in the volume of trade.** If demand in the deficit country contracts or grows more slowly than that in the surplus country, the volume of exports will increase relative to the volume of imports.
- **A change in relative prices through a change in the exchange rate or a change in domestic prices.** Imports become dearer and exports cheaper if the deficit country's currency falls in value or if inflation is lower in the deficit country than in the surplus country. This will tend to depress the demand for imports and boost exports.

Figure 10.5

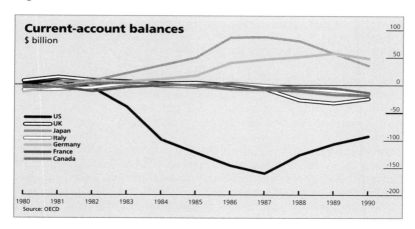

Attempts to regain balance through government export subsidies or import barriers such as quotas or tariffs are essentially imposed volume or price changes (which also cause market distortions). For example, a ban on imports will generate extra, possibly inflationary, demand for domestic goods.

Similarly, trade surpluses may be eroded by faster economic growth, a stronger currency or higher inflation in the surplus country.

CURRENT-ACCOUNT BALANCE

Measures: Net current payments, the difference between national savings and investment.

Significance: Identifies international payments which arithmetically must be matched by capital flows and changes in official reserves.

Presented as: Money total.

Focus on: Trends; size in relation to GDP.

Yardstick: The OECD average current-account balance was −0.6% of GDP during the 1980s.

Released: Usually monthly, quarterly by some countries; at least one month in arrears.

Overview

The current-account balance is the balance of trade in goods and services (see above) plus net rents, interest, profits and dividends (RIPDs) and current transfer payments.

133

Countries which produce monthly current-account figures base their initial estimates on simple projections of previous RIPDs and transfers, which themselves may be revised. Consequently this component of the current account is even less reliable than the goods and services balance and is subject to heavy revision.

Rents, interest, profits and dividends. These reflect past capital flows. Countries (including the Gulf oil exporters) with current-account surpluses acquire foreign assets which generate further current-account income in future periods.

Transfer payments. These include foreign workers' remittances to their home countries, pension payments to retired workers now living abroad, government subscriptions to international organisations and payments of foreign aid.

Host countries with large populations of foreign workers (including Germany) experience transfer outflows. However, for many developing countries workers' remittances save the current account from becoming an unmanageable deficit. Remittances were a particularly important source of foreign currency for poor Arab countries with workers in the rich oil exporting Gulf states during the oil boom years of the 1970s.

Current-account deficits

A visible-trade deficit can be covered by exports of services or net inflows of RIPDs and transfers, but the overall current account cannot remain in deficit indefinitely. It has to be financed by any or all of inward investment, loans from overseas and depletion of official currency reserves.

Direct inward investment in businesses may create new employment, output and exports which should help to eliminate future current-account deficits. Nevertheless capital inflows might be withdrawn at inconvenient times, and they create potential RIPD current-account outflows.

EXTERNAL BALANCES

America's current-account deficit has been shrinking fast. In 1991 it is estimated to have been in rough balance, partly thanks to transfers from foreign governments to help pay for the Gulf war. The OECD forecasts that America's deficit will widen in 1992, to 0.9% of its GDP, but that would still be a fraction of its peak of 3.5% of GDP in 1987. In 1991 Germany had the biggest current-account deficit of any industrial economy; at $21 billion, it represented 1.3% of GDP. As recently as 1990 Germany had the biggest surplus, of $48 billion. After doubling in 1991, Japan's current-account surplus is forecast to widen further in 1992, to $82 billion (2.2% of GDP). As a percentage of GDP, Norway is forecast to have the biggest current-account surplus (5.5%) in 1992, Iceland the biggest deficit (4.3%).

The Economist, January 25th 1992

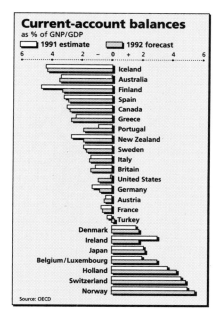

Savings

The current account is sometimes taken as a measure of the gap between domestic savings and investment, although strictly speaking this is measured by the balance of trade in goods and services (see above).

Since government budget deficits represent government dissaving, some commentators argue that if a budget deficit is cut any current-account deficit will fall automatically. This line of reasoning became popular when America developed large current-account and budget deficits in the mid-1980s. The fallacy of the argument was demonstrated when the American current-account deficit subsequently fell without a corresponding reduction in the budget deficit.

The correlation between the budget deficit and the current-account deficit holds good only if private-sector savings and investments remain unchanged, which they generally do not.

Acquisition of net foreign assets

Although the current account does not quite measure net savings, it does measure the net acquisition of foreign assets. In other words, external debt grows by the size of a current-account deficit (see page 134).

CAPITAL-ACCOUNT FLOWS

Measures: International capital flows.
Significance: Major contributor to exchange-rate fluctuations. Outflows represent the acquisition of assets overseas.
Presented as: Money totals.
Focus on: Long-term and short-term movements.
Yardstick: Use current-account balance as indicator.
Released: Quarterly, at least one month after the quarter end. Revised often.

Overview

The capital account records international capital flows. These are frequently neglected by commentators but they are important because they are directly related to the current-account balance and to exchange rates.

Short-term capital movements

Short-term flows into liquid assets such as bank deposits and Treasury bills are easily reversed and are sometimes characterised as "hot money". Since flows can change direction at the drop of an interest rate, they can cause severe volatility in the currency markets.

Long-term capital movements

Long-term capital includes portfolio investment (stocks and shares) and direct investment (such as building a factory overseas). However, it is perhaps increasingly unrealistic to distinguish between investment in stocks and shares (long-term capital) and the acquisition of Treasury bills (short-term capital).

An outflow today implies current-account income in the future. Indeed, with global deregulation, it is easier for companies to raise their market share by setting up production facilities overseas. The initial direct investment shows as a capital-account outflow. Subsequently remitted profits add to current-account inflows and boost GNP relative to GDP. The value of goods sold, however, does not show up in external trade or increase GDP in the way that exports from home would.

OFFICIAL RESERVES

Measures: Gold and foreign currencies held by the government.
Significance: Indicates a country's ultimate ability to pay for imports; signals pressures on the balance of payments.
Presented as: Nominal value at end-month, often in dollars; watch for unrealistic value or revaluation of gold and currencies.
Focus on: Totals and changes.
Yardstick: A crude rule of thumb is that reserves should be sufficient to cover three months' imports. A sudden large change of tens or hundreds of million dollars in one month may indicate exchange-rate pressures.
Released: Monthly; in some countries immediately after the month-end.

Overview

Central banks hold stocks (reserves) of gold and currencies which have widespread acceptability and convertibility, such as the dollar. These reserves are used to settle international obligations and to plug temporary imbalances between supply and demand for currencies.

Intervention

Central banks frequently intervene in the markets to influence their currency's exchange rate. This affects their reserves.

For example, if the Federal Reserve (the American central bank) decides that the dollar is too strong against the yen it may sell (anonymously) dollars in exchange for yen on the open market. The extra supply of dollars creates new demand for yen and tends to depress the exchange rate of the dollar relative to the yen. The Fed increases its foreign currency reserves by the value of the yen purchased.

Conversely, if the Fed thinks that the dollar is too low, it might use its currency reserves to buy dollars and prop up the dollar exchange rate. Intervention in this direction can continue only so long as the central bank has reserves that it can sell.

Central banks might sensibly intervene to smooth erratic fluctuations in currencies, but it is a fool's game to use intervention alone to try to hold a currency at, or move it to, some previously determined level if that is not the level at which market supply and

137

demand are in equilibrium. Such an exchange-rate objective can only be met in the longer term through domestic economic policies (see Exchange rates, page 143).

Sterilisation. When a central bank sells reserves and buys its own currency, the domestic money supply is reduced in size by the amount of domestic currency swallowed up by the bank. Purchases of foreign currencies boost the money supply. Such intervention is said to be sterilised if the central bank neutralises the effect on the money supply with some other action, such as the purchase or sale of government bonds.

Interpretation

Changes in the level of official reserves suggest foreign exchange intervention and, therefore, pressures on the currency:

- a fall in the reserves suggests that there was intervention to offset currency weakness;
- a rise suggests intervention to hold the currency down.

However, reserves change for reasons other than intervention, including government borrowing or payments overseas, and fluctuations in the rates used to convert holdings of gold and currencies into a common unit of account. The total value of reserves can also be misleading if gold is valued at some anachronistic rate, as it frequently is.

Strictly speaking, the level of reserves alone is not a guide to a country's ability to pay its way. That is determined in the short term at least by the government's ability to borrow overseas. If the reserves are running low it is a good idea to look at the country's IMF position (see SDR, page 146), its current level of external debt and its ability to borrow overseas.

EXTERNAL DEBT, NET FOREIGN ASSETS

Measures: Net borrowing by the public and private sectors.
Significance: Liability which can only be repaid from export earnings.
Presented as: Money totals.
Focus on: Total and debt service in relation to exports.
Yardstick: See Table 10.4.
Released: Annually without fanfare.

Overview

Countries which persistently run current-account deficits accumulate external debt. This can become a major problem since essentially the debt repayments and interest can be financed only from export earnings. Table 10.4 indicates the problems for some of the world's largest debtors.

Net foreign assets. Rather than being debtors, many countries, including some industrial countries and oil exporters, have accumulated stocks of assets in other countries. The figures tend to understate the true position due to underdeclaration and book values that are way out of line with market values.

The stock, however, may be of no help for offsetting any current-account deficits. Residents may have no wish to repatriate their assets, especially if the current-account deficit is a signal of fundamental economic problems.

Table 10.4 **External debt, 1989**

	Total debt $m	Debt as % GDP	As % of exports		
			Debt	Debt service	Interest
Largest in $					
Brazil	111	24	302	31	15
Mexico	96	51	264	40	26
Argentina	65	120	537	36	18
India	63	24	259	26	14
Largest relative to GDP and exports					
Mozambique	5	427	1745	23	17
Nicaragua	9	na	2653	9	3

Note: Debt service is interest plus scheduled repayments. Exports cover goods and services.

Source: World Bank

11

EXCHANGE RATES

"Devaluation . . . would be a lunatic self-destroying operation."
Sir Harold Wilson in 1963; in 1967 he devalued the pound.

Exchange rates are nothing more than the price of one currency in terms of another. They are determined mainly by supply and demand, which reflect trade and other international payments, and, much more important, volatile capital flows which are constantly shifting around the world in search of the best expected investment returns.

The prime indicator of market pressures on a currency is the figure for total currency flows in the balance of payments account (see Chapter 10). Other important influences are relative interest rates and yields (Chapter 12) and inflation (Chapter 13).

A history of exchange rates

The easiest way to understand exchange rates and their influence on the balance of payments is to review previous experiences.

The gold standard. Before 1914 exchange rates were fixed in terms of gold, trade was mainly in physical goods and capital flows were limited. A country which developed a deficit on its current account would first consume its reserves of foreign currencies. Then it would have to pay for the imports by shipping gold. The transfer of gold would reduce the money supply in the deficit country and boost it elsewhere, since currencies were then backed by convertibility into gold.

In the deficit country the contracting money supply would tend to depress output and prices. Elsewhere the expanding money supply would boost output and inflation. The deficit country could then only afford to import a lower quantity of dearer foreign goods. The surplus countries could import a higher quantity of the deficit country's cheaper goods. Thus the current account would automatically return to equilibrium.

That was the theory. It seemed to work in practice until the system got out of balance in the 1920s. The gold standard was temporarily suspended during the first world war. Countries experienced rapid and varying rates of inflation and exports were grossly underpriced or overpriced when the gold standard was reintroduced at pre-war rates. Large current-account surpluses and deficits developed. The gold standard fell from favour and was abandoned almost universally by the early 1930s.

The 1930s. There were widespread experiments with fixed and floating exchange rates during the 1930s. Almost every country tried to alleviate the unemployment of the Depression by limiting imports and boosting exports with measures such as import duties, quotas and exchange-rate devaluation or depreciation. It may seem obvious, but world exports cannot rise if world imports fall. The international payments system fell further into disrepute.

Adjustable pegs. An international conference was convened in America at Bretton Woods, New Hampshire, in June 1944. Participants agreed to form the IMF and World Bank to promote international monetary cooperation and the major currencies were fixed in relation to the dollar. Fluctuations were limited to 1% in either direction, although larger revaluations and devaluations were allowed with IMF permission. In addition, the American government agreed to buy gold on demand at just over $35 an ounce, which left only the dollar on a gold standard.

Floating rates. The Bretton Woods system broke down by the 1970s. Persistent American deficits had led to an international excess of dollars and American gold reserves came under pressure. In August 1971 the Americans suspended the convertibility of the dollar, imposed a 10% surcharge on imports and took other measures aimed at eliminating its balance of payments deficit. The major currencies were allowed to float, some within constraints imposed by exchange controls (dirty floats).

Fixed rates with some flexibility were reintroduced in December 1971 following a meeting of the IMF Group of Ten at the Smithsonian Institute in Washington (the "Smithsonian agreement"). However, sterling was floated "temporarily" in June 1972 and by the following year all major currencies were floating or subject to managed floats. Despite bouts of extreme turbulence, most major currencies have remained floating ever since. The exceptions are the currencies of the EC (see EMS, page 149).

NOMINAL EXCHANGE RATES

Measures: Price of one currency in terms of another.
Significance: Influences external trade, capital flows, and so on.
Presented as: Units of one currency for one unit of another.
Focus on: Trends.
Yardstick: Annual movements of more than a few % in either direction can be destabilising.
Released: Minute-by-minute.

Jargon

An exchange rate indicates how many units of one currency can be purchased with a single unit of another. For example, a rate of DM2 against the dollar indicates that 1 dollar buys 2 Deutschemarks; $1 = DM2.

Stronger and weaker. Terminology is based on the currency with the value of 1. If the rate changes from $1 = DM1.50 to $1 = DM3 the dollar has risen or strengthened by 100% against the Deutschemark (it will buy 100% more Deutschemarks). The Deutschemark has fallen or weakened against the dollar, but not by 100% or it would be worthless. It has moved from DM1 = $0.67 to DM1 = $0.33; a drop of 50%.

When currencies get stronger or weaker, they are said to have appreciated or depreciated if they are floating-rate currencies or to have been revalued or devalued if their rates are fixed by the central bank.

Spot rates. Rates for immediate settlement are spot rates.

Forward rates and futures. Exchange rates fixed today for settlement on a given future date reflect nothing more than spot exchange rates and interest rate differentials.

For example, if a bank agrees to buy dollars in exchange for Deutschemarks in one month, essentially it borrows the dollars today, converts them into Deutschemarks, and places the Deutschemarks in the money markets to earn interest for one month. At the end of the month the bank hands over the Deutschemarks, takes the dollars, and uses them to repay the dollar loan. Nobody takes an exchange-rate risk.

Moreover, arbitrage ensures that forward rates, futures and options move in line.

Forward exchange rates and futures should not therefore be regarded as explicit indicators of expected exchange rates.

What determines exchange rates

There is no neat explanation for what determines exchange rates. The two main theories are based on purchasing power and asset markets (investment portfolios).

Purchasing power parity (PPP). The traditional approach to exchange rates says that they move to keep international purchasing power in line (parity). If American inflation is 6% and Canadian inflation is 4%, the American dollar will fall by 2% to maintain PPP. With floating exchange rates this would happen automatically. If exchange rates are fixed, demand pressures will instead equalise inflation in the two countries.

Another version of this, favoured by some economists, is to define purchasing power parity as the exchange rate which equates the prices of a basket of goods and services in two countries. In the long term, it is argued, currencies should move towards their PPP. *The Economist* has a simpler approach with its Big Mac index: this compares the prices of beefburgers sold by a worldwide fast food chain and gives a lighthearted indication of variations in exchange rates and purchasing power.

BIG MacCURRENCIES

The Economist's Big Mac index was first launched in 1986 as a ready reckoner to whether currencies are at their "correct" exchange rate.

The case for munching our way around the globe on Big Macs is based on the theory of purchasing-power parity. This argues that the exchange rate between two currencies is in equilibrium when it equalises the prices of an identical basket of goods and services in both countries. Advocates of PPP argue that in the long run currencies tend to move towards their PPP.

Our basket is simply a Big Mac, one of the few products that is produced locally in a great many countries.

The Big Mac PPP is the exchange rate that leaves hamburgers costing the same in each country. Comparing the current exchange rate with its PPP gives a measure of whether a currency is under- or overvalued.

For example, the average price of a Big Mac in four American cities is $2.19. In Japan our Big Mac watcher had to fork out ¥380 ($2.86) for the same gastronomic delight. Dividing the yen price by the dollar price gives a Big Mac PPP of $1=¥174. On April 10th the actual dollar exchange rate was ¥133, which implies that on PPP grounds the dollar is 24% undervalued against the yen.

The Economist, April 18th 1992

143

The hamburger standard

Big Mac prices Country	Prices* in local currency	Implied PPP** of the dollar	Actual exchange rate 10/4/92	% over(+) or under(-) valuation of dollar
Argentina	Peso3.30	1.51	0.99	−34
Australia	A$2.54	1.16	1.31	+13
Belgium	BFr108	49.32	33.55	−32
Brazil	Cr3,800	1,735	2,153	+24
Britain	£1.74	0.79	0.57	−28
Canada	C$2.76	1.26	1.19	−6
China	Yuan6.30	2.88	5.44	+89
Denmark	DKr27.25	12.44	6.32	−49
France	FFr18.10	8.26	5.55	−33
Germany	DM 4.50	2.05	1.64	−20
Holland	Fl 5.35	2.44	·1.84	−24
Hong Kong	HK$8.90	4.06	7.73	+91
Hungary	Forint133	60.73	79.70	+31
Ireland	I£1.45	0.66	0.61	−8
Italy	Lire4,100	1872	1,233	−34
Japan	¥380	174	133	−24
Russia	Rouble58	26.48	98.95†	+273
Singapore	S$4.75	2.17	˙1.65	−24
S.Korea	Won2,300	1,050	˙778	−26
Spain	Ptas315	144	102	−29
Sweden	SKr25.50	11.64	5.93	−49
United States††	$2.19	—	—	—
Venezuela	Bs 170	77.63	60.63	−22

Source: McDonald's * prices may vary locally, ** Purchasing-power parity: local price divided by dollar price, † Market rate, †† New York, Chicago, San Francisco and Atlanta

Portfolio balance. The portfolio approach suggests that exchange rates move to balance total returns (interest plus expected exchange-rate movements). If Deutschemark deposits pay 6% and dollar deposits pay 8%, investors will buy dollars for the higher return until the exchange rate has been pushed up so far that the dollar is expected to depreciate by 2%. The expected return from the dollar will then exactly match the expected return from the Deutschemark.

Overshooting. The best guess is that exchange rates are determined by PPP in the long run, but that this is overridden in the short term by portfolio pressures. These tend to cause currencies to overshoot PPP equilibrium.

Who determines exchange rates

Clearly there is a complex interaction between exchange rates and various economic and financial variables, many of which are outside domestic control (they are determined exogenously). Central banks can either try to control these variables in order to fix their exchange rate, or leave the exchange rate to the markets.

In fact, of the 150 or so main currencies, fewer than 30 are freely floating, including those of Australia, Canada, Japan, Switzerland and America. The other countries in *The Economist 13* participate in the European exchange-rate mechanism (ERM, see page 149), except for Sweden which pegs its currency to the ecu anyway.

Of the remaining currencies, 30 have managed floats or limited flexibility, while around 30 are pegged to the dollar, 14 to the French franc, five to other single currencies and 40 to the SDR (see page 146) or other baskets of currencies.

Monetary policy. All economic policies affect exchange rates, although changes in interest rates have probably the most direct and visible influence. The exchange rate is thus the broadest indicator of monetary policy.

Intervention. Central banks frequently intervene in the currency markets. They buy or sell their currency in order to alter the balance of supply and demand and move the exchange rate. This is essentially a short-term smoothing activity since they can buy one currency only if they have another to sell. (See Reserves, page 137.)

Effects of exchange-rate movements

The most immediate effect of a weaker currency is higher domestic inflation due to dearer imports. At the same time exports priced in foreign currencies and inflows of rents, interest, profits and dividends generate less income in domestic-currency terms. Thus the trade and current-account balances deteriorate.

Later, after perhaps as much as 12–18 months, relative price movements cause a shift from imports to domestic production and exports. This boosts GDP and the trade and current accounts improve. (Their deterioration followed by improvement is known as the J-curve effect.) However, higher inflation caused by a weaker currency can wipe out any current account improvement within a number of years.

Capital account. With regard to the capital account of the balance of payments, a weaker currency makes inward investment look more attractive. In foreign-currency terms outlays are lower and

145

returns are higher, but this may not be enough to attract investors if the currency weakened because of unfavourable domestic economic conditions.

Table 11.1   **Exchange rates**
Currency units per US$; period averages

Country	Currency	1960	1968	1974–79	1980–90	1990
Australia	dollar	0.89	0.89	0.82	1.19	1.28
Belgium	franc	49.86	49.93	35.16	42.90	33.42
Canada	dollar	0.97	1.08	1.06	1.25	1.17
France	franc	4.90	4.95	4.59	6.57	5.44
Germany	D-mark	4.17	3.99	2.29	2.19	1.62
Holland	guilder	3.77	3.62	2.41	2.45	1.82
Italy	lira	620.9	623.4	782.9	1380.9	1198.1
Japan	yen	359.91	360.55	263.92	194.00	144.79
Spain	peseta	60.11	69.68	66.96	122.59	101.93
Sweden	krona	5.17	5.17	4.37	6.55	5.92
Swiss	franc	4.32	4.32	2.32	1.85	1.39
UK	pound	0.36	0.42	0.50	0.61	0.56
SDR		1.00	1.00	0.83	0.85	0.74
ECU		na	na	0.76[a]	0.98	0.79

[a] 1978–79.

Source: IMF

SPECIAL DRAWING RIGHTS (SDR)

Measures: The value of a basket of five major currencies, see Table 11.2.
Significance: Stable international currency and reserves asset.
Presented as: Absolute value per unit of currency.
Focus on: Market rate against any currency.
Yardstick: Average: $1 = SDR1.19 for 1980–90 and SDR1.36 for 1990.
Released: Several times daily.

Overview

The SDR (special drawing right) is slowly gaining acceptance as a world currency. It was introduced by the IMF in 1970 to boost world liquidity after the ratio of world reserves to imports had fallen by half since the 1950s. Through book-keeping entries, the Fund allocated SDRs to member countries in proportion to their quotas (see below). Countries in need of foreign currency may obtain them from other central banks in exchange for SDRs.

Advantages. The SDR is stable. It is used for accounting purposes by the IMF and even some multinational corporations. Commercial banks accept deposits and make loans in SDRs, and it is used to price some international transactions.

Disadvantages. Since the SDR is an average of five currencies it is less valuable than the strongest and is among the first to go when reserves are sold off. Developing countries argue that it would help their liquidity if they had more SDRs, but the quota system ensures that the rich industrial countries have most of them.

Value

SDRs were first allocated in 1970 equal to $\frac{1}{35}$ of an ounce of gold, or exactly $1 ($1.0857 after the dollar was devalued in 1971). When the dollar came off the gold standard the SDR was fixed from 1974 in terms of a basket of 16 currencies. This proved too unwieldy and in 1981 the basket was slimmed to five major currencies with weights broadly reflecting their importance in international trade (see Table 11.2).

Since 1981 the IMF has paid the full market rate of interest on the SDR, based on a weighted average of rates paid by the individual constituents.

Table 11.2 **Currencies in the SDR**
%

Country	Currency	1981–85	since 1986
USA	dollar	42	42
Germany	D-mark	19	19
Japan	yen	13	15
France	franc	13	12
UK	pound	13	12

Note: Weights based on relative export shares in the period 1975–79 (first column) and 1980–84 (second column).

Source: IMF

Quotas

The IMF allocates to each member country a quota which reflects the country's importance in world trade and payments. The size of the quota determines voting powers, subscriptions in gold and currencies, borrowing powers and SDR allocations.

Any member with balance of payments difficulties may swap its

SDRs for reserve currencies at IMF-designated central banks. It can
also use its own currency to buy (draw) foreign currency from the
Fund's pool. The first chunk of currencies (the reserve tranche),
amounting to 25% of the member's quota, may be taken uncondi-
tionally. Four additional credit tranches each worth another 25% of
the quota may be taken under progressively tougher terms and conditions. When these options are used up there are other borrowing
facilities available. The IMF also arranges standby credits in times of
severe strain on a currency.

Table 11.3   **SDR exchange rates**
Currency units per SDR, period averages

Country	Currency	1960	1968	1974–79	1980–90	1990
Australia	dollar	0.89	0.89	1.00	1.43	1.74
Belgium	franc	49.86	49.93	42.54	50.22	45.34
Canada	dollar	0.97	1.08	1.29	1.49	1.58
France	franc	4.90	4.95	5.57	7.71	7.39
Germany	D-mark	4.17	3.99	2.77	2.56	2.19
Holland	guilder	3.77	3.62	2.92	2.87	2.47
Italy	lira	620.9	623.4	950.3	1624.5	1625.4
Japan	yen	359.91	360.55	319.01	227.27	196.43
Spain	peseta	60.11	69.68	81.29	144.07	138.29
Sweden	krona	5.17	5.17	5.31	7.72	8.03
Switzerland	franc	4.32	4.32	2.80	2.17	1.88
UK	pound	0.36	0.42	0.61	0.72	0.76
USA	dollar	1.00	1.00	1.21	1.19	1.36

Source: IMF

Figure 11.1

EMS, ecu and ERM

Measures: The ecu measures the value of a basket of European currencies.
Significance: Reserve asset, international currency and basis for EC exchange-rate mechanism (ERM).
Presented as: Number of currency units for I ecu.
Focus on: Strongest and weakest currencies in the ERM.
Yardstick: Divergence indicators approaching 75% signal foreign exchange intervention or change in economic policies (see text).
Released: Daily.

Overview

The European monetary system (EMS) is a grand scheme involving a European currency unit (ecu), an exchange-rate mechanism (ERM), credit arrangements and a European Monetary Fund (EMF).

The ecu

The ecu was introduced on March 13th 1979 initially with the same value as the old European unit of account (EUA) which it superseded. While the EUA was no more than a common unit for book-keeping purposes (dating back in various forms to 1962), the ecu is a reserve asset and a currency in its own right used for commercial transactions and bond issues.

Table 11.4 **Ecu exchange rates**
Currency units per ecu; period averages

Country	Currency	1980–90	1988	1989	1990
Australia	dollar	1.25	1.51	1.39	1.63
Belgium	franc	43.62	43.53	43.44	42.54
Canada	dollar	1.32	1.45	1.30	1.48
France	franc	6.70	7.05	7.03	6.93
Germany	D-mark	2.24	2.08	2.07	2.01
Holland	guilder	2.50	2.34	2.34	2.32
Italy	lira	1411.1	1540.9	1512.6	1525.3
Japan	yen	200.69	151.71	152.09	184.33
Spain	peseta	124.83	137.91	130.50	129.77
Sweden	krona	6.71	7.25	7.11	7.53
Switzerland	franc	1.90	1.73	1.80	1.77
UK	pound	0.63	0.66	0.67	0.71
USA	dollar	1.06	1.18	1.10	1.27

Source: IMF

149

The ecu is based on a basket of EC currencies weighted according to the relative size of GDP and trade volume. Weights vary as currencies move, but the German currency has a weight of about 30%, France's is near 20%, Britain, Holland and Italy are each around 10% and the rest are each below 10%.

The ERM

The exchange-rate mechanism links the eleven participating currencies together; the Greek drachma is included in the ecu but does not take part in the ERM.

Each ERM currency has a fixed central rate against the ecu. This is used to calculate a "parity grid" of cross-rates between each pair of currencies. Central banks are required to keep their own currencies within 2.25% of all cross-parities (6% for the Portuguese escudo, Spanish peseta and pound sterling). This effectively means that the strongest currency cannot rise more than 2.25% (6% for the escudo, peseta and sterling) above its central rate against the weakest currency and all other currencies must remain in the band between the two.

A divergence indicator for each currency shows its percentage deviation from its central parity in ecus. The currency with the largest indicator is furthest from the rest of the ERM. If the deviation exceeds 75% the currency's central bank is required to take early corrective action.

Table 11.5   **The ERM**

Country	Currency	Ecu central rates	Ecu market rates	% Change from central rate	% Spread against weakest currency	Divergence indicator
Spain	peseta	133.631	128.636	−3.74	5.92	64
Portugal	escudo	178.735	175.668	−1.72	3.74	27
Belgium	franc	42.4032	42.0849	−0.75	2.73	37
Holland	guilder	2.31643	2.30333	−0.57	2.54	28
Germany	D-mark	2.05586	2.04543	−0.51	2.48	33
Ireland	punt	0.767417	0.767287	0.02	1.98	1
Italy	lira	1538.24	1541.34	−0.20	1.76	−9
France	franc	6.89509	6.92788	0.48	1.48	−26
Denmark	krone	7.84195	7.93656	1.21	0.75	−55
UK	pound	0.696904	0.710570	1.96	0.00	−39

Note: Ecu rates indicate the amount of currency bought for 1 ecu as at April 10th 1992; on that date $1 = 1.2593 ecu. Central rates are changed relatively infrequently by the European Commission. Percentage changes are for ecu; a negative change indicates a strong currency.

Sources: EC; Financial Times

Credit arrangements

The credit arrangements provide for ERM members to borrow reserves if necessary so that they can intervene to support their currencies.

The EMF

The European Monetary Fund (a mini-IMF) was planned for 1981 but it was still not off the ground a decade later.

Other Euro-jargon

The snake. In March 1972 EC members first introduced their own exchange-rate system to provide currency stability within Europe following the collapse of the Bretton Woods system (see page 141). Members agreed to keep their currencies within a 2.25% band which in turn was kept within 4.45% of the dollar (the snake in a tunnel). The tunnel was demolished in 1973 and the snake was left to float against the dollar. Various countries left the snake at various times and it turned into a sort of Deutschemark bloc. In 1979 the snake was reborn as the EMS/ERM.

The green pound. The common agricultural policy (CAP) attempts to stabilise farm prices throughout the EC. Agricultural products are priced in ecu. To avoid price fluctuations due to market-driven exchange-rate movements, conversion into national currencies is at representative (green) rates fixed by administrative decision from time to time. There are different representative rates for different products. In addition, monetary compensatory amounts (MCAs) are imposed as taxes or paid as subsidies to even out prices and avoid distortions caused by relative exchange-rate movements between green fixings. It was the European Commission's objective to abolish green rates and MCAs by 1992.

Eurocurrencies. When the cold war began in the 1950s, Eastern bloc countries transferred dollar deposits to Europe to prevent them from being frozen in New York. The first transfer was by the then Soviet Union to a French bank whose telegraphic address was Eurobank. Dollar deposits outside America became known as Eurodollars and use of the prefix euro has since become widespread. Any currencies held outside of their country of origin, such as dollars or yen in London, are now known as Eurocurrencies.

EFFECTIVE EXCHANGE RATES

Measures: Average exchange rate against a basket of currencies.
Significance: Shows overall exchange-rate movements.
Presented as: Index numbers.
Focus on: Trends.
Yardstick: An increase indicates a strengthening currency. Movements of more than a few percentage points a year can be destabilising.
Released: Daily.

Overview

An effective exchange rate (EER) measures the overall value of one currency against a basket of other currencies. Changes indicate the average change in one currency relative to all the others.

Effective exchange rates are weighted averages of many currency movements with weights chosen to reflect the relative importance of each currency in the home country's trade. For example, if the dollar appreciates by 10% against the Japanese yen but is unchanged against all other currencies, and if the yen accounts for 25% of American trade, the dollar's effective exchange rate has risen by 2.5%.

For obvious reasons EERs are sometimes known as trade-weighted exchange rates. There are many ways of selecting the weights, based on imports of manufactured goods, total trade, and so on.

MERMs. Most indices use weights from the IMF's multilateral exchange-rate model (MERM). This tries to measure the effect of exchange-rate changes on prices of exports and imports, and the response of trade flows to such price changes.

Main sources. The IMF, the major central banks and some other organisations calculate effective rates for all the major currencies. The Bank of England indices published in *The Economist* and some daily newspapers are based on the IMF's model. Most EERs are presented in index form, although sometimes they are shown as the percentage change since a chosen base date.

Interpretation

If, for example, the effective exchange rate for the dollar rises by 1%, this indicates that the various exchange-rate changes that have taken place are the same as a flat 1% rise in the dollar against every individual currency. In other words, the observed movements will have the same effect on the American trade balance as a 1%

overall rise in the dollar.

Effective exchange rates do not take account of inflation so they do not reveal anything about changes in a country's competitiveness (see Real exchange rates below).

Table 11.6   **Effective exchange rates**
Based on IMF MERM; period averages; 1985 = 100

Country	Currency	1985	1986	1987	1988	1989	1990	1985–90
Australia	dollar	100.0	83.9	80.7	87.8	91.2	85.3	88.1
Belgium	franc	100.0	106.2	111.2	110.1	108.4	115.1	108.5
Canada	dollar	100.0	90.3	90.0	95.2	101.0	99.3	96.0
France	franc	100.0	106.0	108.6	106.3	103.9	112.1	106.2
Germany	D-mark	100.0	110.8	119.2	118.4	116.3	124.5	114.9
Holland	guilder	100.0	110.9	118.8	118.6	115.8	122.6	114.5
Italy	lira	100.0	104.0	105.7	101.9	101.7	106.5	103.3
Japan	yen	100.0	126.6	136.9	151.8	145.2	130.1	131.8
Spain	peseta	100.0	102.2	104.5	107.6	110.5	118.8	107.3
Sweden	krona	100.0	101.2	102.2	102.2	101.3	102.3	101.5
Switzerland	franc	100.0	112.5	121.3	119.8	111.6	122.6	114.6
UK	pound	100.0	93.0	92.7	97.7	94.3	94.7	95.4
USA	dollar	100.0	81.9	72.2	68.0	71.0	66.4	76.6

Source: IMF

Figure 11.2

Changes in effective exchange rates
annual average percentage change, 1979–90

153

REAL EXCHANGE RATES; COMPETITIVENESS

Measures: International competitiveness.
Significance: Indicative of a country's ability to sell abroad and of net price (inflation and exchange rate) pressures on the balance of payments.
Presented as: Index numbers.
Focus on: Trends.
Yardstick: The lower the index, the more competitive the country.
Released: Monthly, one month in arrears.

Overview

A country's international competitiveness depends on relative movements in costs or prices after adjusting for exchange-rate movements. For example, if prices increase by 4% in Germany and 6% in America, American competitiveness appears to have fallen by 2%. However, if over the same period the dollar fell by 3%, overall American competitiveness has actually improved by 1%.

Such measures of overall competitiveness are known as "relative costs or prices expressed in a common currency" or, more simply, real exchange rates.

Indicators of prices and costs

There is no ideal measure of competitiveness. Those in common use are listed below. They are described in terms of America, but the calculations are the same for any country.

Relative export prices. American export prices divided by a weighted average of competitors' export prices, all expressed in a common currency. This might seem to be a logical basis for assessing price competitiveness but there are several drawbacks. Such an exchange rate covers only goods that are traded; it does not take account of competition between imports and domestic production in home or overseas markets; it measures orders but ignores unsuccessful quotations; and it fails to take account of profitability (exporters in general are price-takers; they may be forced to absorb exchange-rate movements in profits).

Relative export profitability. American export prices divided by American producer prices. This is not a measure of international competitiveness, but it is a useful supplement to relative export prices. It indicates the extent to which changes in export prices reflect changes in the profit margins on exports against home sales. If export prices rise less rapidly than domestic prices, export profitability has declined.

Import price competitiveness. American producer prices divided by American import prices. This provides a guide to import competitiveness, but again it ignores relative profitability.

Relative producer prices. American producer prices divided by a weighted average of competitors' producer prices. This compares home prices with prices that they will be competing against overseas. It tends to overemphasise domestic markets.

Relative consumer prices. American consumer prices divided by a weighted average of competitors' consumer prices. This ignores capital and intermediate goods, but it is good for comparing relative consumer purchasing power.

Relative GDP value-added deflators. The American GDP deflator divided by a weighted average of competitors' GDP deflators. This is the most comprehensive basis for comparison, covering unit labour costs and profits per unit of output. One drawback is that some of the items in GDP are not traded, although it might be argued that inflation pressures are ultimately transmitted uniformly through all goods and services. Another problem is that the deflators are available only after a sizeable lag.

Relative unit labour costs. An alternative to price competitiveness is to look at cost competitiveness. This has the advantage of covering all industries: exporters, potential exporters and those competing with imports. However, due to a lack of data the only sensible

Table 11.7 **Real effective exchange rates**
Relative normalised unit labour costs; period averages; 1985=100

Country	Currency	1985	1986	1987	1988	1989	1990	1985–90
Australia[a]	dollar	100.0	87.5	87.3	96.1	103.1	100.5	95.8
Belgium	franc	100.0	104.5	105.5	101.0	99.4	102.0	102.1
Canada	dollar	100.0	93.7	99.8	112.5	130.2	139.4	112.6
France	franc	100.0	99.4	97.2	95.0	92.7	96.6	96.8
Germany	D-mark	100.0	111.3	121.3	122.3	121.4	129.1	117.6
Holland	guilder	100.0	105.4	109.8	108.5	103.7	105.6	105.5
Italy	lira	100.0	100.6	102.9	101.9	110.2	117.0	105.4
Japan	yen	100.0	122.9	128.4	137.8	131.1	115.5	122.6
Spain	peseta	100.0	101.6	105.7	112.8	122.0	128.8	111.8
Sweden	krona	100.0	101.6	103.6	108.1	116.4	120.4	108.4
Switzerland	franc	100.0	105.5	107.7	103.8	94.9	97.4	101.5
UK	pound	100.0	94.2	94.0	99.9	98.7	99.2	97.7
USA	dollar	100.0	79.0	66.7	61.2	61.8	55.7	70.7

[a] Relative consumer prices.

Source: IMF

155

indicator is relative unit labour costs (say, American ULCs divided by a weighted average of competitors' ULCs, all in a common currency). This excludes profits and prices of materials.

Normalised relative unit labour costs. These are relative unit labour costs adjusted to allow for short-term deviations in productivity from long-term trends. This smooths out differences in the cyclical position of the countries being compared, but because of the difficulties of adjusting productivity for the cycle it should be treated with care.

Interpretation

Common practice. Relative unit labour costs in manufacturing and relative export prices are the most popular measures, partly because they are available quickly and easily. However, rather than relying on just one indicator it is a good idea to look at several to get a feel for "average" changes.

The indicators are expressed in index form. The index rises if domestic costs or prices increase faster than foreign costs or prices. Thus a larger index number (stronger real exchange rate) indicates that the home country is less competitive. The broad implication is that to restore competitiveness, the currency must weaken or domestic prices/costs will have to increase less than foreign prices/costs.

Current international practice uses 1985 as a base for index numbers. The dollar was particularly strong in that year, and the indices must be interpreted with this in mind.

The indices do not take account of non-price factors (product differentiation) such as quality, reliability and design.

Figure 11.3

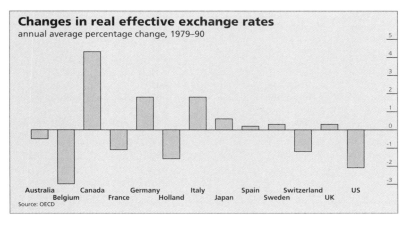

Changes in real effective exchange rates
annual average percentage change, 1979–90

Australia   Canada   Germany   Italy   Spain   Switzerland   US
    Belgium   France   Holland   Japan   Sweden   UK
Source: OECD

TERMS OF TRADE

Measures: The ratio of export prices to import prices.
Significance: Measures the volume of imports that can be bought with one unit of exports.
Presented as: Index numbers.
Focus on: Changes in the index.
Yardstick: An improvement indicates that export earnings will buy more imports – but the trade balance may worsen.
Released: Monthly.

Overview

The terms of trade indicate the purchasing power of a country's exports in terms of the imports that they will buy.

Favourable or unfavourable. The terms of trade are said to improve if export prices rise more rapidly or fall more slowly than import prices. For example, if export prices rise by 5% and import prices rise by 2%, a given volume of exports buys roughly 3% more imports; the terms of trade have improved by 3%.

Common terminology suggests that movements in the terms of trade are "favourable" or "unfavourable". However, after an "unfavourable" movement in the terms of trade, the trade balance will tend to improve (the smaller rise in export prices than import prices means that exports are more competitive), while a "favourable" movement in the terms of trade may price exporters out of the market and result in a weaker trade balance (see Trade balance and Exchange rates, pages 130 and 143).

Which way is up? Governments usually define the terms of trade as export prices divided by import prices expressed in index form. A rise in the index indicates an improvement in the terms of trade – one unit of exports will buy more imports. Academics sometimes do it the other way around, as import prices divided by export prices. The lower the number, the fewer exports needed to obtain one unit of imports. The message is the same in both cases, but you need to check the basis for the calculation before you can interpret the numbers.

Unit value or average values. Terms of trade indices constructed using import and export unit value indices (see Export and Import prices, page 194) are not affected by changes in the commodity breakdown of imports or exports. Terms of trade indices based on average value indices reflect changes in composition as well as changes in prices.

157

In general unit values are most commonly used and are a satisfactory basis for the terms of trade, but where there has been a structural shift in the composition of trade average value indicators are better. For example, if a country imported a larger proportion of oil in 1980 than in 1990 and if oil prices rise, a unit value terms of trade indicator based on 1980 weights will overstate the deterioration in the terms of trade. An average value indicator will show a smaller, more realistic, deterioration.

Devaluation or depreciation. Typically, an exchange-rate devaluation or depreciation increases import prices relative to export prices and causes the terms of trade to deteriorate.

12

MONEY AND FINANCIAL MARKETS

*"There have been three great inventions since the beginning of time:
fire, the wheel and central banking."*
Will Rogers

Money

The cornerstone of the modern economy is money, which is a measure of value, a medium of exchange and a store of wealth. It is also the bridge between real and nominal magnitudes, so understanding it is vital for understanding and controlling inflation.

Markets

Financial markets bring together the supply of savings and the demand for money to finance businesses and consumer spending. The markets also allow people to complete commercial transactions and spread risks. Note that there are two sides to every transaction: for every lender there is a borrower; for every seller, a buyer.

Interest rates

Interest rates are the price of money. They link large stocks of physical and financial assets with smaller flows of savings and investment; they connect the present and the future; and they are sensitive to inflation expectations. As a result they are very volatile and hard to predict. With all these factors at work, it is hardly surprising that there is no simple theory which explains why interest rates behave as they do.

Liberalisation and globalisation

Financial systems changed dramatically in the 1970s and 1980s. There were three main influences.

- **Liberalisation and deregulation.** Exchange, credit and

interest rate controls were abolished or relaxed in the major industrialised countries.

- **Innovation.** Many new financial instruments and derivatives were introduced, including financial futures and options.
- **Technological change.** Computers, telephones and facsimiles (fax) allow transactions to be completed quickly and cheaply.

As a result the world's major financial markets became much more integrated. A change in American, Japanese or German interest rates is felt immediately throughout the world, which means that domestic monetary policies are influenced by uncontrollable outside influences. Monetary variables are harder to control and the demand for money is less sensitive to domestic interest rates.

Key figures

The following briefs examine money and bank lending, interest rates, bond yields and share prices. They are all interlinked. Nevertheless perhaps the widest indicator of monetary conditions is the exchange rate (see page 140).

MONEY SUPPLY, MONEY STOCK, M0 ... M5, LIQUIDITY

Measures: Notes, coins and various bank deposits.
Significance: Indicator of level of transactions and, perhaps, inflation or output.
Presented as: Money totals at a point in time, usually end-month; except averages of Wednesdays for Canada and daily averages for Japan and America.
Focus on: Changes over time.
Yardstick: OECD average broad money growth was 9.6% a year during the 1980s.
Released: Monthly; one month in arrears.

Overview

Money is anything which is accepted as a medium of exchange; essentially currency in circulation plus bank deposits. Notes and coin, issued by the monetary authorities (mainly central banks) account for only a tiny proportion of the money supply. The rest is bank deposits which are initially created within the banking sector.

The total amount of money in circulation, the money stock or money supply depending how you look at it, is often called M.

The number of times it changes hands each year is its velocity of circulation, V.

Multiply the two together (M × V) and you have the amount of money that is spent, which by definition must equal real output Y multiplied by the price index P; that is, M × V = Y × P.

This equation is the basis for understanding money. Assume for the moment that velocity is fixed or predictable (it is not particularly). In this case, argue the monetarists, controlling the money supply controls money GDP (that is, Y × P); and if the trend in real output Y can be predicted inflation can be controlled. Their opponents argue that cause and effect run in the other direction, that money GDP fixes the demand for money and there is nothing that can be done about it.

Whoever is right, if you are prepared to accept that velocity is fixed in the short term, then as a dangerously crude rule of thumb, subtract the inflation rate from the rate of growth of money to estimate the growth of real output.

Money defined

Narrow money, M1. Narrow money is fairly uniformly defined as the non-bank private sector's holdings of notes, coin and sight deposits (chequeing accounts where cash is available on demand). In shorthand this "aggregate" is called M1. Notable variations among *The Economist 13* are as follows.

- Germany includes deposits that can be withdrawn on up to one month's notice.
- Britain's narrow money measures are M0 (see below) and M2 which includes building society deposits (there is no longer an M1).
- America includes travellers' cheques and other chequeable deposits.

Broad money, M2. This is M1 plus time and savings deposits and foreign currency deposits of residents other than central government. Notable variations are as follows.

- Australia and Italy include certificates of deposit (CDs).
- Belgium includes CDs and investments in unit trust funds.
- Britain's broad-money measure is called M4 and includes building society deposits; the national definition of M2 is narrower, while M3 is no longer published.
- France includes various money market instruments.
- Holland includes Treasury bills.
- Japan focuses on a measure called M2 + CDs, which is self-explanatory.

- America's M2 is M1 plus overnight repurchase agreements and Eurodollar deposits held by American residents at branches of American banks worldwide and all banks in Britain and Canada; general purpose and broker/dealer money market mutual fund balances; and savings and small time deposits.

M3. Wider still, M2 is M2 plus other liabilities of financial institutions. For example, American M3 is M2 plus term repurchase agreements and Eurodollar deposits; institution-only money-market mutual fund balances; and large time deposits.

The following table appears in this format weekly in *The Economist*.

MONEY AND INTEREST RATES   The 12-month growth in Canada's broad money supply stayed at 5.7% in January; its narrow-money growth quickened to 6%. In the year to December Italy's broad-money growth rose to 9.1%; and its narrow money growth to 10.5%.

| | money supply‡ | | interest rates % p.a. (February 18th 1992) | | | | | | | |
| | % rise on year ago | | money market | | commercial banks | | bond yields | | eurocurrency | |
	narrow [M1]	broad	overnight	3 months	prime lending	deposits 3 months	gov't long-term	corporate	deposits 3 months	bonds
Australia	+10.3	+ 2.1 Nov	7.35	7.30	11.75	7.30	10.05	11.21	7.50	na
Belgium	+ 6.3	+ 5.3 Q2	9.40	9.60	13.25	9.60	8.75	9.04	9.63	8.76
Canada	+ 6.0	+ 5.7 Jan	7.50	7.39	7.50	7.15	9.19	10.07	7.13	8.79
France	− 5.1	+ 3.2 Dec	10.75	9.94	10.35	9.88	8.52	9.22	9.94	8.54
Germany	na	+ 5.7 Dec†	9.65	9.50	11.00	8.65	8.04	8.12	9.63	7.64
Holland	+ 5.2*	+ 5.2* Nov	9.25	9.58	11.75	9.58	8.31	9.35	9.63	8.36
Italy	+10.5	+ 9.1 Dec	12.25	12.31	13.00	na	10.96	11.06	11.88	10.17
Japan	+ 8.6	+ 2.0 Dec	5.56	5.21	5.88	2.75	5.38	5.70	5.44	5.46
Spain	+15.2	+12.0 Dec	12.73	12.81	16.00	8.50	10.81	11.68	12.50	10.97
Sweden	na	+ 4.1 Dec	12.10	12.27	13.50	12.30	9.73	11.94	12.25	10.74
Switzerland	+ 1.1	+ 3.1 Nov	7.38	7.38	9.38	6.88	6.18	6.69	7.38	6.62
UK	+ 2.8	+ 6.2 Dec	10.81	10.31	11.50	10.22	9.18	10.47	10.28	9.73
USA	+ 8.6	+ 1.5 Dec	4.81	4.14	6.50	4.07	7.98	8.63	4.13	6.68

Other key rates in London 3-mth Treasury Bills 9.7%, 7-day Interbank 10.5%, clearing banks' 7-day notice 4.0%. Eurodollar rates (Libor): 3 mths 4.1%, 6 mths 4.3%. † % change from 4th quarter at annual rate. * New series.

‡ M1 except UK M0; M3 except Belgium, Holland, Italy and Sweden M2, Japan M2 plus CDs, Spain M3 plus other liquid assets, UK M4. Definitions of interest rates quoted available on request. Sources: Banco Bilbao Vizcaya, Chase Manhattan, Banque de Commerce (Belgium), Credit Lyonnais, Bank Nederland, Royal Bank of Canada, Svenska Handelsbanken, Westpac Banking Corp, CSFB, The WEFA Group. These rates cannot be construed as offers by these banks.

Money: other variations

Monetary base. Some countries pay particular attention to the monetary base (see reserve assets and monetary control below).

- Britain's M0 is almost entirely cash in circulation, but it also includes banks' operational deposits at the Bank of England.
- Germany's CBMS (central bank money stock) is currency in circulation plus banks' required minimum reserves held at the central bank. This was the main target variable until 1987.

Liquidity. Many countries also watch total holdings of liquid assets, which include a wider range of instruments and are less affected when funds are moved around in response to changes in relative interest rates. Notable measures include the following.

- Britain. PSL (private sector liquidity) covers currency, deposits, savings instruments, and wholesale money-market funds.
- France. Total liquidity is M3 plus short-term negotiable assets issued by non-banks and contractual savings schemes managed by credit institutions.
- Spain. ALP (total liquidity) is M3 plus mortgage securities, Treasury bills, bankers' acceptances, commercial paper and Bank of Spain deposit certificates (ALP = liquid assets in the hands of the public).

Velocity of circulation

Velocity of circulation, that is, the number of times money changes hands in a year, may be measured by nominal GDP divided by any monetary aggregate such as M2 averaged over the year.

Deposit creation and monetary growth

Commercial banks create money. They can lend out a large proportion of deposits placed with them, since it is unlikely that all customers will ask for their money back at once.

Suppose a bank receives a new $100 deposit and lends $80 of it. By the stroke of a pen the bank creates a loan (debit balance $80) and a new deposit (credit balance $80). Even if the customer withdraws the entire $80 to pay for some consumer goods, the retailer is likely to redeposit the $80, probably in a different bank. The second bank has a new deposit of which it might lend $60. This credit creation will gradually peter out, but not until one new deposit has created loans (= deposits = money) of several times its own size.

Reserve assets

For prudence and monetary control central banks limit the proportion of new deposits which banks can on-lend by requiring them to hold a fixed proportion of their assets in the following.

- **High powered reserves.** Cash (till money) and balances at the central banks (operational deposits) which are used to meet day-to-day requirements for customer withdrawals and inter-bank settlements.
- **Secondary reserves.** "Safe" liquid assets such as Treasury bills which can be used to meet temporary increases in withdrawals.

163

Monetary control

Monetary authorities attempt to control the size and growth of money in several ways.

- **Changing reserve-asset ratios.** This affects the multiple which banks can lend and is usually done only once every few years.
- **Open-market operations.** Buying or selling government bonds in the open market, which increases or reduces the amount of money in bank reserves and private deposits.
- **Influencing interest rates.** For example, through open-market operations (which affects the supply and demand for money), changing the discount rate (see page 167), or imposing fixed rates for certain deposits or loans.
- **Credit controls.** For example, limits on total bank lending, total personal credit, or the margins that borrowers have to put up for any credit purchase.
- **Moral suasion.** For example, central banks hold heart-to-heart talks with commercial bankers, perhaps to persuade them to restrict lending.

Note that direct control over reserve-asset ratios and the monetary base affects the supply of money while the other measures affect demand for it.

Alternative indicators of monetary growth

Monetary growth can be tracked by watching the deposits which are included in the various monetary aggregates. Alternative approaches are to track the following.

- **The banking sector's balance sheet.** Movements on the liabilities side (deposits) must be matched by movements in assets (mainly loans) and liabilities not included in monetary aggregates.
- **Sectoral counterparts.** These are measured by money the public sector takes out of circulation (roughly, the budget surplus plus government bond sales to non-banks) plus net additions by the banking sector (mainly bank lending) plus net additions from overseas (net balance of payments inflows to the private sector).

Monetary targets

Monetary authorities adopt many approaches to monetary

control. For example, the US Federal Reserve (the central bank) pays close attention to M2 as an indicator of inflationary pressure. The Fed's broad thinking is that for price stability the long-run growth of M2 should approximately equal the trend growth in output. M2 grew within its 1989 and 1990 target bands of 3-7%. For 1991 and 1992 the target band was reduced to 2.5-6.5%. The Fed also targets M3, but this is considered less important than M2.

Three other examples of monetary practices, focusing on narrow through to broad money, are as follows.

- The British target the monetary base M0, with a range of 0-4% growth set for the financial year to March 1992.
- The Bank of Japan watches M2 + CDs, which was projected to grow by 8% in the year to the first quarter of 1991.
- Germany and France both target broad M3, with ranges of 4-6% and 5–7% respectively for 1991.

Table 12.1 **Money supply**
Annual % change

	Narrow money				Broad money			
	1960 –68	1968 –73	1973 –79	1979 –90	1960 –68	1968 –73	1973 –79	1979 –90
Australia	3.7	11.1	10.5	11.2	7.9	13.4	10.9	14.2
Belgium	na	na	8.4	4.5	na	na	11.2	7.5
Canada	6.2	10.3	8.9	4.8	na	na	17.8	7.6
France	na	na	na	7.7	na	na	na	9.7
Germany	7.8	8.9	9.6	6.3	8.8	13.3	7.3	7.2
Holland	8.4	10.4	9.8	6.6	8.6	12.7	10.2	8.3
Italy	12.3	22.6	18.5	11.2	12.7	17.5	20.6	11.4
Japan	17.3	21.6	9.7	4.9	18.0	20.2	11.9	9.0
Spain	15.2	18.7	16.7	13.1	na	21.5	19.0	11.2
Sweden	na	na	na	na	9.0	9.1	10.5	8.3
Switzerland	7.1	8.7	4.9	2.7	na	na	7.3	5.9
UK	na	na	na	na	na	na	13.4	16.0
USA	4.3	5.9	6.5	7.2	8.5	10.1	10.7	7.7
EC	na	na	na	na	na	na	na	11.6
OECD	na	na	na	na	na	na	na	9.6

Sources: IMF; OECD

Interpretation

Goodhart's law, named after a former Bank of England economist, says that any monetary variable loses its usefulness within six months of being adopted as a target of monetary policy. The problem is that if relative interest rates or other influences change, investors quickly move their balances from deposits with one institution (which might be included in a particular definition of money) to another (which might not). This can cause the Ms to jump up and down at different rates and make interpretation tricky. Other complications include international capital flows and changes in the velocity of circulation.

Watch for cash lurking in the sidelines and changes in domestic and international relative interest rates and yields, and for factors which might distort some or all monetary aggregates.

Many monetary measures are seasonally adjusted, but be on the lookout for erratic influences. It is advisable to take several months together or the target period to date and compare with the same period a year earlier.

In general, if the target aggregate is growing too rapidly expect the central bank to raise interest rates. If money is growing below target, there might be scope for lower interest rates.

BANK LENDING, ADVANCES, CREDIT, CONSUMER CREDIT

Measures: Loans to persons, companies and the public sector.
Significance: Indicator of monetary conditions.
Presented as: Monthly totals.
Focus on: Trends.
Yardstick: Roughly, growth should equal target for monetary aggregates.
Released: Monthly; one month in arrears.

Overview

Changes in overall bank lending figures indicate the effectiveness of monetary policy. Changes in lending to various sectors may indicate trends in various parts of the economy.

Personal and consumer credit

Net new borrowing by households finances the purchase of homes and consumer goods and services. Such borrowing tends to be sensitive to interest rates and consumer confidence. It is translated directly into higher spending (see also Retail sales, House sales, Motor vehicle sales, Consumer expenditure), output and imports.

Growth in household credit is generally good when demand is slack, but can be inflationary when demand is already buoyant. Excessive borrowing to finance the acquisition of other financial assets such as shares is also worrying: it may help to drive up their prices, making consumers feel more wealthy and ready for a bout of inflationary spending.

Borrowing by companies

Companies borrow to finance their operations, investment and takeovers. Corporate borrowing generally slackens when the economy is booming and funds are generated by buoyant sales. On the other hand, there will be more investment activity when companies are most optimistic (see Business conditions, page 103).

A breakdown by industry will reveal trends in various industrial sectors. High borrowing may reflect either optimism and investment or recession and debts. Output, orders and capacity utilisation figures will indicate which.

CENTRAL BANK DISCOUNT, LOMBARD, INTERVENTION RATE

Measures: Interest rates at which central banks lend to banking systems.
Significance: Indicator of central banks' monetary policy; influences banks reserves, monetary growth and market interest rates.
Presented as: Annual percentage rate.
Focus on: Rate, trends.
Yardstick: See Table 12.2.
Released: Changed daily, fixed weekly, or moved only at irregular intervals.

Overview

Within the constraints of market pressures, central banks manage their banking systems to keep liquidity and short-term interest rates at or near to officially desired levels (see also Money supply, page 160). Central banks:

- intervene in the interbank money market to manage the daily balance of supply and demand;
- often publish formal discount rates at which they provide money to commercial banks to help smooth longer (say, weekly) financing needs; and
- occasionally impose penal rates for emergency lending to banks.

In general discount rates have more of a psychological importance than a direct influence over market rates and the cost of money

167

(see below). Central banks tend to implement their policies by intervening in the markets to control an implicit or explicit target such as the Fed funds rate in America and call money in Japan (see Interest rates, page 169).

Intervention rate

The intervention rate is the rate at which the central bank intervenes in the interbank market to manage day-to-day liquidity. France and Spain have formal intervention rates which are changed only irregularly.

Other countries have less formal systems and add liquidity when necessary at a rate which is appropriate to supply, demand and the official interest rate policy. Watch the seven-day advances rate in Belgium; the special advances rate in Holland; and central bank (overnight government bond) repo rates in many other countries including Germany and America.

Repo. This is a sale and repurchase agreement where one financial dealer sells, say, bonds to another with agreement to buy them back at a given price on a given date.

The discount rate

Specifically, the discount rate is the rate at which central banks discount (buy), rediscount, or lend against eligible paper. Such finance typically has a maturity of up to 1–2 weeks.

Eligible paper. This ranges from Treasury notes in Australia to a whole range of industrial and commercial paper, Treasury bills and Treasury bonds in America.

Quantity. There are usually limits on the quantity of paper that can be discounted. Additional borrowing is at penal rates based on the discount rate (for example, Italy and Sweden) or identified separately (the German Lombard rate).

Rate. The discount rate is usually set by administrative decision. Two notable exceptions are as follows.

- Canada. The rate for temporary advances to chartered banks and for repos with money-market dealers is set at 0.25% above the average rate on 3-month Treasury bills.
- Sweden. The rate charged to commercial banks on short-term loans varies according to whether banks meet established liquidity and cash ratios and whether advances to the private sector exceed prescribed credit ceilings.

Other names. The discount rate is called the central bank rate in Belgium and the Bank of Spain rate in Spain. Of *The Economist* 13, Britain alone has no discount rate or equivalent. The old minimum lending rate (MLR) or base rate was abolished in the 1980s to take the political heat out of the government's interest rate policy. The Bank of England still controls the rate for short-term funds by intervening and MLR has been reintroduced occasionally during liquidity crunches.

Interpretation

Central bank intervention can give advance warning of changes in its interest rate policies. Some central banks hold regular policy meetings (for example, the fortnightly meetings of the Bundesbank Council and the Fed open market committee, FOMC).

Note that discount rates tend to follow money-market interest rates, which themselves are influenced by central bank intervention. They may also set a floor for other rates, otherwise banks will "round-trip" by borrowing "at the discount window" and reinvesting the cash at a higher rate in the money markets.

INTEREST RATES; SHORT-TERM AND MONEY-MARKET RATES

Measures:	Interest charged on financial paper with maturity up to 12 months.
Significance:	Indicator of monetary conditions, expectations, creditworthiness.
Presented as:	Annual percentage rates (see also discount rates above).
Focus on:	3-month interbank (or CD/Treasury bill rate if no interbank rate).
Yardstick:	See Tables 12.2 and 12.4.
Released:	Almost continuously around the clock.

Overview

Money markets are the markets in which banks and other intermediaries trade in short-term financial instruments.

The hub is usually the interbank market (called the Federal funds market in America), which is where banks deal with each other to meet their reserve requirements (see Money supply, page 160) and, longer-term, to finance loans and investments.

Very short-term interbank interest rates are largely determined by central bank intervention (see page 167), although market pressures are also influential. For other maturities and other financial instruments, relative maturities and credit risks are also important.

Figure 12.1

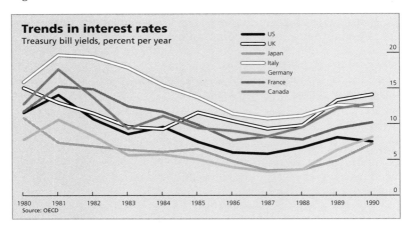

Maturity. Loans in the short-term market range from call (repayable on demand) and overnight to 12-month money. Interest rates on 12-month paper are higher than on shorter maturities if market participants expect interest rates to rise, or lower if rates are expected to fall. Supply and demand imbalances can cause temporary interest rate bulges at various maturities. It is not unknown for overnight money to top 100% on rare occasions. Use 3-month rates as the benchmark.

Credit risk. Treasury bills (loans to the government) are regarded as completely safe in the major industrial countries and command the finest (lowest) interest rates, usually below interbank rates. Interest rates are higher on certificates of deposit (CDs – bank deposits which can be sold) and, usually, higher still on corporate or commercial paper (loans to companies).

LIBOR and variants

Interbank rates are quoted bid (to borrow) and offer (to lend). The London interbank offered rate (LIBOR) is a benchmark. The interest rates on many credit agreements worldwide are set in relation to it; for example, as LIBOR plus 0.5%.

Most major financial centres have LIBOR equivalents, such as AIBOR, FIBOR and PIBOR in Amsterdam, Frankfurt and Paris.

There is no direct equivalent in America. Its interbank market is the Federal funds market, while the base for loan contracts is the prime rate (the rate charged to borrowers with prime or excellent creditworthiness). However, whereas LIBOR changes constantly under direct influence of supply and demand, the prime rate is set by the banks (with reference to market rates) and is changed less regularly.

Two technical points

Interest and discount. Note the difference between interest rates (investment yields) and discount rates. Treasury bills and commercial paper are issued at a discount to their maturity value. A 12-month bill with a face value of $100 might be sold for $92.50, when the discount is $7.50:

- the discount rate is 7.5% (7.50 divided by 100 as a percentage);
- the interest rate is 8.1% (7.50 divided by 92.50 as a percentage).

Basis points. Dealers sometimes talk about basis points, where 100 basis points = 1% (percentage point) or 1 basis point = 0.01%.

Interest rates and the economic cycle

Whether by government action or by constraints of supply and demand, interest rates tend to rise when economic activity is buoyant and fall when it is slack.

Lower interest rates encourage borrowing, which leads to more consumer spending and investment, increased imports, a higher level of economic activity and possibly faster inflation. Higher interest rates do the opposite. The problem for finance ministers and central bankers is getting the timing right. It can take perhaps 12-18 months for the full effect of a change in interest rates to feed through.

Interest rates and currencies

Changes in interest rates affect the relative attractiveness of holding a currency (see Exchange rates, page 142). For example, an increase in American interest rates will encourage a shift into the dollar, pushing it up and making American imports cheaper and European imports dearer. Other countries which want to maintain exchange-rate relationships or prevent money-market outflows are forced to raise their interest rates as well.

Figure 12.2

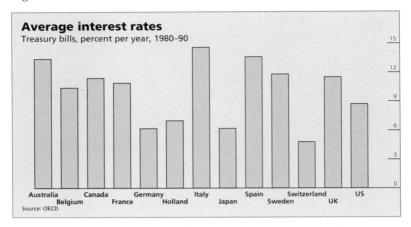

Average interest rates
Treasury bills, percent per year, 1980–90

Australia   Canada   Germany   Italy   Spain   Switzerland   US
    Belgium   France   Holland   Japan   Sweden   UK
Source: OECD

Table 12.2   **Central banks and comparative interest rates**
% per annum, 1990 averages

	Discount	3-month IB[a] deposit[b]	primes[c]	Loan/ primes[c]	Treasury bills[d]	Gov't bonds[e]
Reserve Bank of Australia	15.24	14.15	15.29	21.69	16.80	13.18
Banque Nationale de Belgique	10.50	9.63	6.13	13.00	9.62	10.06
Bank of Canada	11.78	12.73	12.81	14.06	12.81	10.85
Banque de France	9.50	10.32	6.68	17.00	10.16	9.96
Deutsche Bundesbank	6.00	8.49	7.07	11.59	8.10	8.88
Nederlandsche Bank	7.25	8.68	3.31	11.75	8.09	8.93
Banca Italia	12.50	12.06	6.79	14.08	12.38	11.51
Bank of Japan	6.00	6.93	3.56	6.95	na	7.36
Banco de Espana	14.71	15.15	10.65	16.01	14.17	14.68
Sveriges Riksbank (Bank of Sweden)	11.50	13.66	9.93	17.18	13.66	13.08
Banque Nationale Suisse	6.00	8.84	8.28	7.42	8.32	6.68
Bank of England	na	14.77	6.22	14.75	14.08	11.08
US Federal Reserve	6.50	8.10	8.16	10.01	7.51	8.55

Note: Rates are end-year for all discount rates and for bonds in Australia, Belgium, France, Japan and Switzerland.

[a] Interbank rates, except Australia (bank-accepted bills), Italy (interbank sight), Japan (Gensaki), Switzerland (Eurodeposits) and USA (Fed funds, end-year).
[b] Rates banks pay on term deposits (CD rate for USA).
[c] Rates banks charge prime customers.
[d] 3-month except Germany (12 months).
[e] Government bonds are 10-year (20 for the UK) except where only shorter maturities are in issue.

Source: OECD

BOND YIELDS

Measures: Interest return on fixed-interest securities.
Significance: Indicator of interest and inflation expectations, credit-worthiness.
Presented as: Annual percentage rates.
Focus on: Long-dated government bonds.
Yardstick: See Table 12.3.
Released: Almost continuously around the clock.

Overview

Bonds are loans with fixed regular coupons (interest payments) and usually a fixed redemption value on a given date. Some bonds are perpetual or undated loans which are never repaid or are repaid only at the borrower's option.

The yield (effective rate of interest) on bonds is determined by market conditions. Investors in bonds want to be compensated for loss of interest on other instruments, the time and credit risk of holding bonds and expected inflation. Risks are minimised with government bonds (loans to the government) and unlike shares the maturity value is fixed, so the yield on long-dated government bonds may be taken as an indicator of expected trends in interest rates and inflation.

British government bonds are known as gilts, or gilt-edged securities, after the paper on which they were once printed.

Yield calculations

Bonds are traded in secondary markets at prices which in a mechanical sense reflect their redemption value, coupon, credit rating and other interest rates.

For example, a closely watched American Treasury (government) bond with an 8.125% coupon repayable at $100 in 2008-11 was trading at just under $103 in late 1991. In return for the $103 outlay, a buyer would receive $8.125 a year in coupons and $100 on maturity, making the effective investment yield, or rate of interest, 7.3% a year.

Corporate bonds with the same maturity and redemption details trade at a lower price (higher yield) reflecting the greater risk of default.

Benchmark bonds that professional investors watch are shown in Table 12.3. These change over time as bonds mature and new ones are issued.

Yields and prices. Note the negative relationship between bond

173

yields and bond prices. If prices fall, interest yields increase. If prices rise, interest yields decline.

Yields and the economic cycle

Since interest rates tend to rise when economic activity is buoyant and fall when it is slack, bond prices tend to fall on the upward leg of the economic cycle and rise on the downward leg.

Index-linked issues

The British and some other governments have issued index-linked bonds, where the coupons and redemption value are linked to consumer prices. The yield on such bonds is the real interest rate.

For example, in late 1991 the real yield on index-linked gilts was roughly 4% (depending on inflation assumptions) while the yield on long-dated conventional gilts was 9%, implying expected inflation of 5% a year.

However, such calculations should be regarded with suspicion, because the volume of index-linked bonds is so small that individual trades can move the market.

Table 12.3 **Benchmark government bonds**
Prices and yields on December 31st 1990

	Coupon %	Redemption date	Price local currency	Yield %
Australia	13.00	July 2000	105.17	12.07
Belgium	10.00	August 2000	99.60	10.05
Canada	10.50	March 2001	101.35	10.26
France	9.00	November 1995	95.39	10.23
	8.50	March 2003	91.19	9.99
Germany	9.00	October 2000	100.00	8.99
Holland	9.25	November 2000	100.25	9.21
Japan No.119	4.80	June 1999	88.11	7.04
No.129	6.40	March 2000	98.35	6.69
UK	9.00	March 2000	89.44	10.84
	9.00	October 2008	88.81	10.38
USA	8.50	November 2000	102.87	8.06
	8.75	August 2020	105.56	8.24

Source: Financial Times

YIELD CURVES, GAPS AND RATIOS

Measures: Difference between interest yields on different instruments.
Significance: Indicator of interest and inflation expectations.
Presented as: Annual percentage rates.
Focus on: Long-dated government bonds and other interest rates.
Yardstick: See Table 12.4.
Released: Almost continuously around the clock.

Overview

Various yield differentials signal market perceptions of risks, interest rates, inflation and perhaps exchange-rate movements. You can focus on the difference between any two yields. Four common measures are described below.

Yield curve

Strictly speaking, the yield curve is a line on a graph linking interest rates for a whole range of maturities. However, it can be represented numerically by the difference between two maturities, such as the yield on long-term government bonds less 3-month money-market interest rates.

Long rates are usually higher than short rates to allow for the time and inflation risks of holding bonds. However, the curve flattens or inverts when monetary conditions tighten, mainly because of the increase in short rates. The curve may therefore be used as a signal of monetary conditions and a leading indicator of economic activity.

Yield differential

The yield differential is the gap between bond yields in two countries. For example, it might be defined as American less German long-term government bond yields, in which case a narrowing of the differential indicates a reduction in the relative attractiveness of the dollar. (See Interest rates and Exchange rates, pages 169 and 143.)

Yield gap or reverse yield gap

The yield gap is the yield on long-term government bonds less the average dividend yield on shares. Decades ago, before the markets were worried about inflation, the yield on shares was higher than that on bonds (that is, the gap was negative), reflecting the greater risk of holding equities. The gap is now generally positive (sometimes called a reverse yield gap) because investors demand a higher return from bonds to compensate for the inflation risk of holding instruments with fixed redemption values. The gap therefore says something about expected inflation (and the relative attractiveness of bonds and shares – see yield ratio).

Yield ratio

The yield ratio is the yield on long-term government bonds divided by the average dividend yield on shares. The yield ratio was between 2 and 4 in each of the major markets in the early 1990s, except in Japan where it moved between 8 and 11. Loosely, a high ratio relative to historical experience in the country in question implies that equities are overvalued relative to bonds.

Table 12.4   **Yields**
% per year

	Treasury bills[a]		Gov't bonds[b]		Yield curve[c]	
	1974–79	1980–90	1974–79	1980–90	1974–79	1980–90
Australia	8.3	13.3	9.7	13.6	1.4	0.3
Belgium	8.3	10.4	8.8	10.6	0.5	0.2
Canada	8.6	11.4	9.2	11.6	0.6	0.2
France	9.2	10.9	9.5	11.6	0.3	0.7
Germany	5.7	6.2	7.7	7.7	2.0	1.5
Holland	7.8	6.9	8.7	8.3	0.9	1.4
Italy	13.2	14.6	12.8	14.2	−0.4	−0.4
Japan	7.7	6.2	8.0	6.6	0.4	0.4
Spain	11.6	13.6	na	14.4	na	0.8
Sweden	7.2	11.8	9.4	12.1	2.1	0.3
Switzerland	2.4	4.8	4.9	4.9	2.5	0.1
UK	10.3	11.5	13.6	11.2	3.3	−0.4
USA	6.9	8.7	8.1	10.4	1.2	1.7

[a] Rates are 3-month except Germany (12-month); other money-market rates for Japan; Holland pre-1975; Italy and Spain pre-1977; Switzerland pre-1979; and France pre-1986.
[b] Yields are long-term, generally over ten years but two years for Spain.
[c] Bond yields less bill rates.

Source: IMF

REAL INTEREST RATES AND YIELDS

Measures: Any interest rate or yield less the rate of inflation.
Significance: Determinant of investment behaviour.
Presented as: Per cent per year.
Focus on: 3-month money, long-dated government bonds.
Yardstick: See Table 12.5.
Released: Almost continuously around the clock.

Overview

Real interest rates are nominal interest rates deflated by the rate of inflation. For simplicity, this may be approximated by subtraction. For example, over the period 1980–90 American 3-month interest rates averaged 8.7% and consumer prices rose by 5.5% a year, so the real interest rate was about 8.7 − 5.5 = 3.3%.

Implicitly at least, investment decisions are based on real interest rates. Since inflation over the period ahead is unknown, it is the expected real interest rate that influences behaviour. This cannot be measured easily, so the latest rate of consumer-price inflation is usually used as a proxy when calculating real interest rates.

Interpretation is tricky. Logic suggests that high real rates will discourage physical investment, but recent studies suggest that cause and effect run in the opposite direction; it is the demand for investment funds that makes real interest high in the first place.

Table 12.5 **Real yields**
% per year; interest rates and yields less consumer prices

	Treasury bills		Gov't bonds		Yield curve	
	1974–79	1980–90	1974–79	1980–90	1974–79	1980–90
Australia	−3.6	5.1	−2.3	5.3	1.4	0.3
Belgium	−0.0	5.6	0.5	5.8	0.5	0.2
Canada	−0.6	5.1	−0.0	5.3	0.6	0.2
France	−1.4	4.0	−1.2	4.7	0.3	0.7
Germany	1.1	3.3	3.1	4.8	2.0	1.5
Holland	0.6	4.1	1.5	5.5	0.9	1.4
Italy	−2.9	3.9	−3.3	3.6	−0.4	−0.4
Japan	−2.2	3.7	−1.8	4.0	0.4	0.4
Spain	−6.3	3.8	na	4.6	na	0.8
Sweden	−2.5	3.7	−0.4	4.0	2.1	0.3
Switzerland	−1.6	1.3	0.9	1.4	2.5	0.1
UK	−5.3	4.0	−2.0	3.6	3.3	−0.4
USA	−1.7	3.3	−0.5	4.9	1.2	1.7

Note: See footnotes to Table 12.4.

Source: IMF

SHARE PRICES AND YIELDS

Measures: Prices of company share capital.
Significance: Reflect economic expectations; useful as a leading indicator.
Presented as: Individual prices in money and indices of average prices.
Focus on: Broad market indices.
Yardstick: See Table 12.6.
Released: Almost continuously around the clock.

Overview

Share prices reflect the discounted value of future dividend payments, with a premium thrown in to reflect the risks. Future dividends depend on company profits, which in turn reflect the quality of management and the state of the economy. For the stockmarket as a whole, variations in management quality average out, leaving perceptions about the state of the economy as a key factor in determining overall share prices.

When investors expect recession, they are less keen to buy equities and their prices fall (a bear market). As soon as there is a glimmer of economic recovery, investors switch into equities, pushing up their prices (a bull market). Thus share prices are highly cyclical, and act as valuable leading indicators of expectations.

Table 12.6   **Share prices**
Annual % change

	Nominal share prices				Real share prices			
	1960 −67	1968 −73	1974 −79	1979 −90	1960 −67	1968 −73	1974 −79	1979 −90
Australia	2.3	6.0	2.4	12.2	0.2	0.9	−8.5	3.7
Belgium	−2.6	8.6	−5.1	10.4	−5.2	3.9	−12.4	5.4
Canada	8.9	6.6	2.1	7.6	6.6	2.0	−6.5	1.2
France	−4.2	8.7	1.0	14.4	−7.3	2.6	−8.8	7.0
Germany	−3.6	3.8	−0.1	10.0	−6.2	−0.2	−4.5	7.0
Holland	−2.6	7.3	−4.2	12.1	−6.3	0.9	−10.6	9.1
Italy	−5.1	0.4	−9.1	19.4	−9.0	−4.4	−21.7	8.0
Japan	1.8	21.9	3.7	15.4	−3.6	14.1	−5.7	12.5
Spain	5.7	20.4	−15.7	17.3	−1.3	12.9	−28.5	6.8
Sweden	3.2	5.8	2.9	24.5	−0.8	0.5	−6.2	15.1
Switzerland	−4.4	7.6	−2.9	7.6	−7.7	2.5	−6.6	4.0
UK	2.4	8.2	6.3	14.6	−1.0	1.1	−8.0	6.5
USA	7.6	3.3	−0.8	11.8	5.8	−1.5	−8.6	6.0

Note: Industrial share prices, daily averages except France and Switzerland (end-week), Canada and Sweden (end-month) and Belgium (10th day of each month).

Source: IMF

Broad indices and sectors

For economic fortune-telling, focus on broad market indices which average out erratic influences. For example, use the American Standard and Poor's 500 stock index rather than the Dow Jones Industrial Average of 30 stocks; and the British FT (*Financial Times*) all-share index of nearly 700 shares rather than the FTSE (*Financial Times* Stock Exchange, or Footsie) index of 100 shares.

Sector averages, such as indices for consumer goods or building materials' companies, should be used to assess market expectations for various parts of the economy.

SHARE PRICES

Morgan Stanley Capital International's World Index is weighted according to the market value of 1,504 companies in 20 countries. In January 1990 Tokyo-listed companies accounted for the largest share of the index, with a collective weight of 39%. By the end of July 1991, thanks to tight monetary policy, a (slightly) weaker yen and some startling financial scandals, this had fallen to 30%. American firms' share of the global equity market rose from 31% to 37%, helped in recent months by better company results and signs of economic recovery. Europe's share of the market increased from 24% to 28%. Despite fcalling earlier this year, by September 3rd the world index stood 8.2% higher in dollar terms than a year before.

The Economist, September 7th 1991

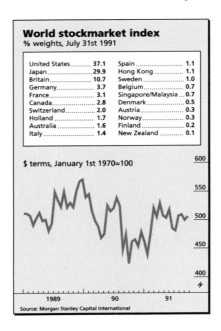

World stockmarket index
% weights, July 31st 1991

United States	37.1	Spain	1.1
Japan	29.9	Hong Kong	1.1
Britain	10.7	Sweden	1.0
Germany	3.7	Belgium	0.7
France	3.1	Singapore/Malaysia	0.7
Canada	2.8	Denmark	0.5
Switzerland	2.0	Austria	0.3
Holland	1.7	Norway	0.3
Australia	1.6	Finland	0.2
Italy	1.4	New Zealand	0.1

$ terms, January 1st 1970=100

Source: Morgan Stanley Capital International

179

13

PRICES AND WAGES

"Inflation means that your money won't buy as much today as it did when you didn't have any."
Anon

Overview

Price indicators tell you about inflation. An increase in the general level of prices is nothing new: records from the days of the Roman Empire show rapid inflation. Since 1946 Britain's consumer prices have risen every year, but in fact inflation – in the sense of continuously rising prices – is historically the exception not the rule. Linking together various price series (of admittedly varying quality) suggests that in 1914, on the eve of the first world war, British consumer prices were no higher than during the 1660s. During those 250 years periods of rising prices were interspersed with periods of falling prices.

Inflation has three main adverse effects. First, it blurs relative price signals; that is, it is hard to distinguish between changes in relative prices and changes in the general price level. This distorts the behaviour of individuals and firms, and so reduces economic efficiency. Second, because inflation is never perfectly predictable, it creates uncertainty, which discourages investment. Third, inflation redistributes income: from creditors to borrowers, and from those on fixed incomes to wage-earners.

Some economists contend that inflation of 2–3% a year is a natural and unavoidable condition of a healthy, growing economy. Others believe that price stability should be the goal of central banks. The Reserve Bank of New Zealand, for example, has an explicit target of reducing inflation to 0–2% by 1993.

Causes of inflation

There are two main theories about the causes of inflation; supply-shock and demand-pull. The reality is probably a complex mixture of the two.

Supply-shock (or cost-push). Prices are pushed up by higher wage and raw material costs; perhaps due to trade union power, dearer imports as a result of a weak currency, or a jump in commodity prices.

Demand-pull. Prices are pulled up when spending power (demand) is greater than the availability of goods and services. Factors which can boost aggregate demand include tax cuts, higher government spending, wage rises caused by labour shortages and an increase in consumer borrowing.

Recent experiences

Experiences with inflation range from deflation (a fall in prices experienced, for example, during the 1930s depression and by some oil-producing countries in the mid-1980s) to hyperinflation (such as when German wholesale prices rose by about 1.5 trillion % between 1919 and 1923). Hyperinflation is frequently associated with rapid increases in the money supply (see Chapter 12).

Industrial countries. Inflation was moderate in the industrial world in the 1960s, averaging about 3% a year. It jumped sharply after the two oil price shocks in the 1970s before falling again in the 1980s. In the fight to tame inflation, wage and price controls have generally given way to tight monetary and fiscal policies.

Developing countries. Inflation generally accelerated in the

Figure 13.1

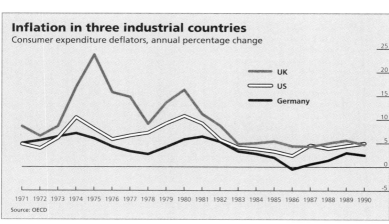

Inflation in three industrial countries
Consumer expenditure deflators, annual percentage change

UK
US
Germany

1971 1972 1973 1974 1975 1976 1977 1978 1979 1980 1981 1982 1983 1984 1985 1986 1987 1988 1989 1990

Source: OECD

181

developing countries in the 1980s, due mainly to lax economic policies. Experiences varied. Bolivia's unremitting monetary and fiscal squeeze from 1985 brought annual inflation down from 24,000% to 10% by 1988. On the other hand, Argentina's price and wage freeze, with the introduction of a new currency pegged to the dollar, had only a temporary effect. Annual inflation fell from 1,000% to 80% in about a year, before climbing back above 100% as a result of trade union pressures and the government's failure to control its budget.

> The world has turned upside down. In Germany and Switzerland, long seen as bastions of sound money, infla-tion has soared. Yet Australia and New Zealand, so often afflicted by high inflation, now boast the lowest rates in the OECD. Over the year to the fourth quarter of 1991, New Zealand's consumer prices rose by only 1% and Australia's by 1.5% – their lowest inflation rates in 30 years.
>
> Have they discovered a magic cure down under? Alas, no; their success in taming inflation is mainly the result of old-fashioned tight money, with painful effects on output and jobs. In each country the government is trailing badly in the opinion polls, and politicians have been under pressure to stimulate the economy before elections next year.
>
> *The Economist*, March 7th 1992

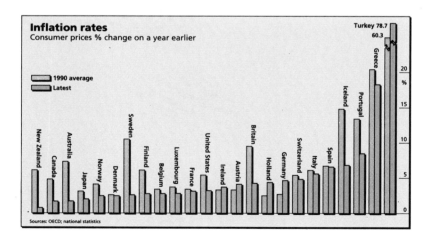

Inflation rates
Consumer prices % change on a year earlier

Table 13.1   Comparative inflation rates, 1960-90
Annual % change

	Hourly earnings	Prod- ucer prices	Con- sumer prices	Consumption private	gov't	Invest- ment	Exports ↕ G&S[a]	Imports G&S[b]	GDP
Australia	7.6[a]	7.6[a]	6.9	7.1	7.9	7.2	5.8	6.1	7.2
Belgium	8.4	3.3	4.9	5.0	5.6	5.0	4.4	4.5	5.0
Canada	7.1	4.6[a]	5.6	5.3	6.8	4.5	4.5	4.0	5.4
France	9.8	5.4	6.6	6.9	8.1	6.6	5.5	6.0	6.9
Germany	6.9	2.8	3.5	3.5	5.1	4.0	2.9	2.6	4.0
Holland	2.9[a]	1.9[a]	4.5	4.6	6.7	4.9	3.0	2.9	5.0
Italy	13.2	9.1[a]	9.0	9.3	11.9	9.9	8.2	8.5	9.8
Japan	9.7	0.9[a]	5.6	5.3	7.3	3.4	1.3	2.8	4.8
Spain	12.3[a]	8.1[a]	10.2	10.1	12.1	9.6	8.6	7.9	10.2
Sweden	8.5[a]	7.4[a]	6.9	7.3	8.5	6.8	5.9	6.5	7.2
Switzerland	5.2	2.3	3.9	4.1	5.0	3.9	3.1	2.2	4.5
UK	10.0[a]	7.6	8.0	7.6	9.4	7.8	7.0	6.8	8.1
USA	5.3	4.3	5.1	4.8	5.6	4.4	4.0	5.2	4.9
EC	7.8[a]	6.2[a]	7.2	6.4	8.1	6.5	4.8	4.9	6.6
OECD	5.9[a]	5.3[a]	6.3	5.7	6.9	5.4	4.5	4.9	5.8

Implicit price deflators

Note: Over the same period, 1960–90, annual price increases were: gold, 8.6%; oil, 9.0%; and, as measured by the IMF: food, 3.2%; beverages, 2.2%; agricultural raw materials, 4.6%; metals, 4.1%; and overall non-fuel commodity prices, 3.7%.

[a] 1979–89.
[b] Goods and services. See following briefs for details of the individual series.

Source: OECD

Inflation and the economic cycle

Cycles set in train by supply shocks are evident in Figure 13.1. The analysis of inflation is also aided by an understanding of the effects of the economic cycle, where pressures often come through on the demand side. Prices increase less rapidly or even decline during recession when consumer spending is weak. However, at the top of the cycle when personal incomes are buoyant but businesses cannot increase their output, extra demand pulls up prices.

PRICE INDICATORS

Price indicators measure levels and changes in particular prices or groups of prices. For example, an oil price index covers one set of hydrocarbons while a consumer price index relates to a basket of goods and services purchased by households. In turn, these price series act as leading indicators of cost pressures and also signal movements in current demand. Table 13.1 shows changes in some key price series over the four cycles 1960–90.

Price indices are sometimes called deflators when they are used to convert (deflate) figures in current prices into constant price terms.

The composition of price indices

Most price indices are weighted averages of several prices. It is difficult to choose weights for some indicators, such as commodity price indices (see page 190), although often the basis for the weighting is clear. If 20% of an average family's spending goes on food, food has a 20% weight in the index of consumer prices. This can cause problems for interpretation, since there may not be an average family. The average rate of inflation is not experienced by a newly married couple with spending dominated by mortgage payments, nor by a retired person with little expenditure on consumer durables. It also poses problems if spending patterns are changing over time.

- **Base-weighted indices** may be used to measure changes over any period. A good example is the American GDP fixed-weight price deflator which uses weights relating to 1987. The weights are the same for each year, so changes in the index reflect changes in prices only. The snag is that the weights may become outdated.
- **Implicit deflators** reflect changes in prices and spending patterns. For example, the American GDP implicit price deflator measures the difference between current and constant price GDP. Since the weights reflect the composition of GDP in each period, changes in the index reflect movements in both prices and the composition of GDP.

The transmission of inflationary pressures

When looking at price indicators, think about their relationship to final prices.

Sequence. The briefs on wages and prices are arranged loosely in the order in which inflationary pressures are transmitted through the economy: from raw material prices and wages through producers' selling prices and consumer prices to the GDP deflator. Indicators towards the end of the chapter are also signals of the state of aggregate demand.

Prices in the early stages of production generally fluctuate more than prices at later stages. A 5% change in raw material prices is generally less worrying than a 5% change in producers' selling prices.

Relationships. The sequence of cost pressures is clear, but it is not so simple to identify a fixed relationship between any pair of price indicators.

- There are leads and lags. In general, changes in raw material costs take longer to feed through to retail prices than movements in producers' selling prices.
- The ultimate effect depends on the cost mix. For example, if raw material prices rise by 10% and account for one-tenth of a manufacturer's costs, and if all other costs are held constant, the effect is a 1% increase in list prices.
- Any movement in output prices will reflect the extent to which higher input costs are absorbed in profits or offset by improved efficiency and productivity.

Indicators to use

Consumer prices are the most rapidly available guides to "national" inflation and they can be used as yardsticks for interpreting other price indicators. For example, wage settlements above the rate of consumer price inflation suggest increasing inflationary pressures (unless they are absorbed by productivity growth – see Unit labour costs, page 202).

Cost pressures are signalled by commodity prices, producer prices and wages and earnings. Surveys of price expectations are valuable leading indicators. The GDP deflator itself may be the best overall guide to inflation and should fluctuate least because it covers so many things, but it is available only after a time lag. Share prices and house prices are useful indicators of asset prices, which influence aggregate demand (see Consumer spending, page 83).

For reviewing particular groups of prices or their effect on certain industries or groups of consumers, select an appropriate indicator. For example, to track the cost of capital equipment purchased by a particular industry, look for a sub-index in the producer prices or the GDP investment deflators.

Cross-references. Just about every economic indicator says something about demand pressures. Capacity use and unemployment are particularly useful, as are indicators of the government's monetary and fiscal stance. See also Balance of payments and, particularly, Exchange rates (Chapters 10 and 11).

Rates of change

Remember to distinguish between a fall in the level of prices and a fall in the rate of increase. If the inflation rate declines but remains positive, prices are still rising.

As a rule of thumb, annual inflation of 0-3% is considered good. Double-digit percentage rises are definitely bad news. Negative inflation, although rarely experienced, is not good either since it signals deflation and – almost certainly – a contracting economy.

GOLD PRICE

Measures: Market price of gold.
Significance: Raw material and psychologically important store of wealth.
Presented as: $ per oz.
Focus on: Trends. Use price in SDRs if possible.
Yardstick: Forward prices for 1995 were $400–550 in 1991, implying a 7% a year increase. Investors hope that the price will rise at least fast enough to compensate them for the interest they could otherwise earn on a "safe" bank deposit, after adjusting for any exchange-rate movements.
Released: Continuously around the clock.

Influences on the price of gold

The gold price reflects the interaction of supply and demand in a global market with many buyers and sellers and a free flow of information. Supply depends on production and sales from stocks while demand is influenced by gold's dual function as an industrial raw material and the ultimate store of wealth. It provides a security which cannot always be matched by paper money. Speculative demand is the major short-term determinant of price.

Supply. South Africa is by far the largest producer of gold, followed by the former Soviet Union, North America and Australia. In the past Soviet output has not shown any strong relationship to prices. Other countries' production generally edges upwards in the long run in response to higher prices. Sales of gold from stocks are important since stocks are many times greater than annual production. Even though central banks and the IMF sold gold in the 1970s and 1980s when it fell from favour as a monetary standard, they still hold 940m oz in their vaults. Uncertainty about what they might do with this may depress prices, but central bankers in developing countries will dent their gold hoards and egos only as a last resort.

Demand. Fabrication demand is mainly for jewellery, electronics and dentistry. Jewellery demand accounts for over half of industrial and commercial use and is very sensitive to price. Electronics demand reflects the fortunes of the industry, decreasing during recession. Use in dentistry is fairly constant, if vulnerable to replacement by man-made materials.

Speculative and investment demand is much harder to predict since flows are large in relation to stocks and output. There tend to be flights into gold which push up its price during rapid inflation, exchange-rate turbulence or political instability worldwide. However, these are less marked now that financial markets offer more sophisticated hedging instruments. Indeed, gold-backed financial instruments, such as gold options, have eroded the lure of holding the metal itself.

Forward sales. Financial engineers have also created a wide range of instruments which allow producers to hedge several years' future output. This was probably the most important influence on prices in 1990. Every time prices rose, they were capped as forward sales pushed more metal into the world market. The mining company RTZ estimated that by the end of the year over 1,100 tonnes were sold forward and it expected the total to increase to a plateau in the mid-1990s.

Currency. Since gold is generally priced in dollars it is important to distinguish between exchange-rate effects and underlying price movements. The easiest way to do this is to convert the price into a basket currency such as the SDR. Surprisingly, not many people do this.

Gold as an indicator of inflation

Many economists, especially Americans, argue that gold is a useful indicator of inflationary pressures, but it is difficult to disentangle all the influences on gold prices. Baskets of commodity prices probably make better leading indicators than gold alone. Moreover, it does not make much difference whether gold is included or excluded from such baskets if they are weighted according to world production levels. If gold is given a greater weight to reflect its psychological importance, the predictive value of such baskets deteriorates. In other words, a commodity price index is preferable as a leading indicator of inflation.

OIL PRICES

Measures: Market price of crude petroleum.
Significance: Major energy source essential to every economy; also a chemical feedstock.
Presented as: $ per barrel.
Focus on: Traded crude such as North Sea Brent or West Texas Intermediate.
Yardstick: Around $20 a barrel. Any increase in oil prices beyond a dollar or two a year is potentially damaging for world output and inflation. Rapid price swings are destabilising.
Released: Continuously around the clock.

Prices, supply and demand

Oil prices are sensitive to supply and demand, with OPEC exports being the major determinant of short-term price fluctuations. Table 13.2 shows levels of supply and demand which kept prices around $20 a barrel in 1990 and against which subsequent supply and demand changes can be judged.

Demand. There are obvious seasonal variations in oil demand; consumption always decreases during the hot summer months. However, in the short term annual demand is fixed in relation to GDP. Consumption fluctuates with the economic cycle in industrialised countries and rises relentlessly in line with economic growth in less developed countries. (Since 1973 oil intensity – oil consumption per unit of GDP – has fallen due to conservation and the substitution of other fuels.)

Supply. Oil producers can be divided into three groups: OPEC; the former communist bloc; and what the oil industry calls the free world. Oil output in the free world is price responsive; it becomes profitable to extract oil from marginal fields only when prices are high. Within such considerations the free world normally produces oil flat out. World market sales from the Eastern bloc do not fluctuate wildly in the short term at least. The gap between demand and supply is therefore filled by OPEC crude. The organisation's attempts to control the world petroleum markets led to oil price rises in 1973 and 1979 and a sharp slump in 1986.

In the short term OPEC exports reflect the balance between members' collective willingness to restrict output to try to control the world oil market, their individual need for revenue, and the general political situation in the oil producing countries. More ominously for the longer term, OPEC members are sitting on oil reserves which promise to outlast all other supplies.

Stocks. Whereas almost all the gold ever produced is still in existence (even if some is in orbit or on the sea bed), oil is rapidly consumed. Oil companies and some governments hold working and strategic stocks which help to prevent prices rocketing in times of temporary crisis, such as during the Iraqi invasion of Kuwait in 1990. Stocks of 100 days' forward consumption are about the highest to expect.

Table 13.2 **The world oil market**

	1988	1989	1990	1991	1992[a]	1993[a]
Demand						
OECD consumption	37.5	37.8	37.9	37.8	38.2	38.8
OPEC consumption	4.0	4.3	4.4	4.6	4.9	5.1
USSR[b] consumption	8.9	8.8	8.4	8.2	7.7	7.3
Other	14.2	15.0	15.4	15.5	15.9	16.5
Total	64.7	65.8	66.1	66.1	66.7	67.7
Supply						
OECD production	16.6	15.9	15.9	16.3	16.2	16.0
OPEC production	21.7	23.7	25.1	25.3	25.9	27.4
USSR[b] production	12.6	12.3	11.5	10.4	9.7	9.3
Other	13.7	14.1	14.4	14.7	14.9	15.0
Total	64.6	66.0	66.9	66.6	66.7	67.7
Change in stocks	−0.1	0.1	0.8	0.5	nil	nil
Trade						
OECD net imports	19.5	20.7	21.0	20.4	20.6	21.4
OPEC net exports	17.6	19.3	20.7	20.7	21.0	22.3
USSR[b] net exports	3.7	3.6	3.1	2.2	2.0	2.1
Other net imports	1.9	2.2	2.3	2.2	2.4	2.9
OECD crude import price						
$ per barrel FOB[c]	13.8	16.5	21.3	18.8	19.5	20.0

Note: Totals may not equal sum of components due to rounding.

[a] OECD forecasts.
[b] Former name.
[c] Free on board.

Source: OECD

Traded crude. OPEC's slippery grip on oil trade means that its official selling prices (OSPs) are not necessarily representative of market pressures. However, whereas nearly all oil was sold on long-term contracts at fixed prices in the past, most is now traded at market prices. A traded crude such as North Sea Brent blend is therefore a good indicator of market conditions.

Table 13.3 **Effect of a $3/barrel rise in oil prices**[a]
% change in one year

	USA	Japan	Europe	OECD
Real GDP	−0.1	−0.3	−0.2	−0.2
GDP deflator	0.1	0.3	0.5	0.4
Employment	–	−0.1	−0.1	−0.1
Current account ($bn)	−5	−5	−5	−12

[a] Based on oil at $20 a barrel.

Source: OECD

Economic effects. An increase in oil prices is bad news for consumers everywhere. Table 13.3 indicates the possible effect of a $3 a barrel rise in oil prices. For the industrial countries as a group, such a change would depress real GDP by 0.2%; knock 0.1% off employment; lead to a $12 billion deterioration in the current account of the balance of payments; and add 0.4% to inflation as measured by the GDP deflator. Inflationary effects at the consumer level would be more pronounced since the GDP deflator does not directly reflect changes in import prices.

COMMODITY-PRICE INDICES

Measures: Changes in groups of commodity prices.
Significance: Advance warning of inflationary pressures.
Presented as: Index numbers.
Focus on: Trends in SDR terms.
Yardstick: Prices fluctuate wildly; hope for level trends.
Released: Daily by Reuters; weekly by *The Economist*; others monthly.

Significance

Commodities are unprocessed or semi-processed raw materials used in the manufacture of other goods. Commodity prices in general are important lead indicators of cost pressures. Prices of metals and, to a lesser extent, non-food agriculturals are also indicative of the level of demand in the industrialised countries.

Monetarists note with glee the correlation between high commodity prices and liquidity in the late 1980s, and the monetary contraction and commodity price falls of the early 1990s.

Price instability

Analysis by the World Bank shows that price instability for sugar, the least stable commodity price, is over 11 times greater than that for oranges, the most stable. Moreover, commodity price fluctuations have increased sharply since the 1960s. Quite apart from the eightfold increase in the real price of oil during the 1970s, the prices of other commodities moved sharply. For example, food prices fell while timber prices rose in the 1980s. Many economic problems can be traced to these shocks and the policy responses to them.

Influences on prices

Commodities may be divided into three broad groups depending on whether their prices are influenced mainly by demand, supply, or both.

Demand. The prices of industrial raw materials, such as metals and minerals, fluctuate in response to changes in demand, reflecting mainly economic conditions in the industrialised countries. Recession brings lower demand and weaker prices. Supply tends to be more stable and predictable.

Demand for metals declined as the industrial countries introduced materials-saving technology during the 1970s and 1980s. This process may be continued in the developing countries during the 1990s. However, some analysts warn that environmental pressures could push up the cost of producing metals such as copper and aluminium by 10–15% in the first half of the 1990s.

Supply. Food prices are influenced most heavily by unplanned changes in the supply side. For example, world vegetable oil prices depend significantly on the effects of weather on the American soya bean crop and on policies relating to American stockpiles. Food prices fell in the late 1980s and early 1990s as production and stocks recovered from the 1988 drought in America which cut output and pushed up prices.

Supply and demand. Non-food agricultural products such as cotton and rubber are vulnerable to changes in both supply and demand.

Index composition

Creating an ideal commodity price index is intellectually testing because:

- commodities are not comparable – 1 tonne of coffee is quite different from 1 tonne of copper;
- they are difficult to value – for example, only 2.5% of rice pro-

191

duction is traded on international markets; and
- relative prices are distorted by large fluctuations in individual commodity prices.

Despite these problems there are many indices combining the prices of several commodities. Apart from *The Economist* commodity price index, the most widely followed indices are prepared by the IMF, the UN, the World Bank and the American Commodity Research Bureau (CRB). They differ in three main ways.

The basket contents. *The Economist* index includes only commodities which are freely traded on open markets. This excludes items such as iron ore and rice which have a big weight in the other main indices. *The Economist* also omits oil and precious metals such as gold which account for a quarter of the CRB index. The two previous briefs suggest that gold and oil are important commodities but they are subject to special factors which may make them less valuable as simple cost indicators.

The basket weights. *The Economist* index is designed to measure cost pressures in industrial countries; its constituents are weighted according to their share in OECD imports. The UN, IMF and World Bank indicators are intended to monitor the terms of trade in developing countries; the constituents are weighted to reflect shares in developing countries' exports. The CRB index just gives equal weight to all components, which understates the importance of industrial commodities and so makes it less useful as a leading indicator of inflation.

Figure 13.2

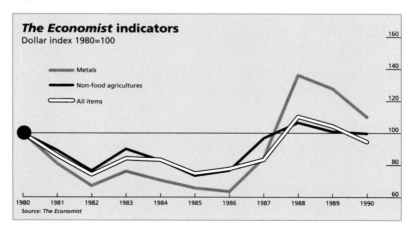

Source: The Economist

192

The currency. Commodity prices are most often quoted in dollars. As a result, currency fluctuations will move indices even when there is no underlying change in commodity prices. An index quoted in SDR terms is better.

COMMODITY PRICE INDEX

Led by a rally in base-metal prices, which rose 10% in two months, *The Economist* all-items dollar index has gained 4% since the beginning of January. The metals rally may not last. Exports from the former Soviet Union are expected to surge in the coming months, after the lifting of export taxes, and world demand is still weak. The non-food agriculturals index has risen 5%, boosted by near-record timber prices in Chicago, and by a recovery in demand for wool. In contrast, the food index slipped 3% in the first seven weeks of 1992. The surge in wheat prices slowed after a lull in Russian buying; and cocoa prices have fallen 10% since mid-January.

The Economist, March 28th 1992

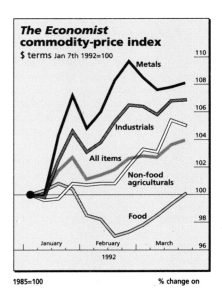

Bottom line

The Economist index in SDRs is hard to beat for tracking the interrelation between cost pressures and inflation; see the weekly commentary in *The Economist*. A rise in the index may signal higher inflation, but the final outcome depends on monetary conditions and supply and demand in other factor markets such as labour.

A UN, IMF or World Bank index should be used if you are interested in the way that changes in commodity prices affect the external balances of developing countries: a fall in commodity prices implies a deterioration in exporters' trade balances.

EXPORT AND IMPORT PRICES; UNIT VALUES

Measures: Prices of traded goods.
Significance: Helps identify cost pressures, potential exchange-rate problems and changes in competitiveness.
Presented as: Index numbers.
Focus on: Changes in unit values (see text).
Yardstick: A positive rate of increase, as close to zero as possible, is good. Check the ratio between import and export prices (see Terms of trade, page 157).
Released: Monthly with trade figures; quarterly with GDP.

Prices. Import or export price indices, including the deflators released with GDP data, capture changes in both the prices and the composition of a country's external trade.

Unit values. Indices of import or export unit values, which are essentially fixed-weight price indices, highlight changes in prices only. This is useful for reviewing cost and competitive pressures. However, since the weights get out of date when the structure of trade changes – as it inevitably does – unit value indices are best for analysing short-term trends.

Export prices or values. Compare export price indices with domestic price indicators, such as the producer price index for home produced goods, to get a feel for the way that manufacturers are passing on cost pressures to foreign buyers; or perhaps being constrained from doing so by international competitive pressures.

Import prices or values. Use import price indices to judge external cost pressures. Import prices that are rising faster than domestic prices are a clear warning of imported inflation.

Erratic items. Remember that the prices of raw materials, including oil, can fluctuate widely and decrease as well as increase. It is often sensible to look at price indices which exclude these more erratic items to identify underlying pressures.

Terms of trade. One of the most useful ways of looking at import and export prices is by examining the ratio between them, which is known as the terms of trade (see page 157).

PRODUCER AND WHOLESALE PRICES

Measures:	Prices of goods at the factory gate.
Significance:	Leading indicator of cost pressures.
Presented as:	Monthly index numbers.
Focus on:	Percentage changes.
Yardstick:	OECD average producer prices rose 5.5% a year during the 1980s.
Released:	Monthly (quarterly in France), at least one month in arrears.

Wholesale price indices (WPIs) cover prices charged at the first stage of bulk distribution and generally include import prices. WPIs were first introduced to measure prices of raw materials.

Producer price indices (PPIs) track prices of home produced goods at the factory gate. Most PPIs cover output prices of goods, although some countries also prepare input price indices for raw materials purchased by industry. In principle, input prices include transport to the factory and output prices are ex-works, although such prices cannot always be identified neatly.

PPIs shed light on cost pressures affecting domestic production and are more useful than WPIs. Most major countries now produce PPIs but Switzerland produces only a wholesale prices index, as do, for example, Austria, Greece and Norway. The indices cover manufacturing and, sometimes, agriculture (Belgium).

Index construction

The indices are compiled on the basket principle with weights reflecting the output of each contributor relative to the total. For example, if lace-makers account for 1% of total industrial production, lace prices have a 1% weight in the index.

Weights are generally updated at 5–10 year intervals to take account of the changing structure of industry, but the Australian weights date back to 1969 and the Swiss weights to 1959–61.

Data are acquired by surveys, usually of major companies. The Swiss index covers 600 price series, the American index over 3,000, and the UK index over 10,000.

In many cases returns are collected continuously so that the prices are effectively monthly averages rather than those applying on just one date. Even so, changes one month will not be reflected fully until the following month.

Taxes such as VAT are usually excluded. Excise duties such as on tobacco and alcohol are treated as manufacturers' costs and are included, so the index moves if they are changed.

The cycle

Prices are generally order prices with list prices adjusted by government statisticians to allow for "normal" discounts in each industry. This is fine when the economy is stable, but the PPI may overstate cost pressures when above-average discounts are offered during a recession. Conversely, the PPI understates cost pressures when inflation is rapid; deliveries may be at prices which were negotiated perhaps several months earlier and which are much below current order prices scored in the index.

Use

Producer output prices and consumer prices tend to follow the same path, with producer prices fluctuating more widely. However, producer prices generally increase less rapidly than consumer prices (compare Tables 13.4 and 13.7).

Table 13.4 **Producer prices for manufacturing**
Annual % change

	1960–68	1968–73	1973–9	1979–89	1989	1990
Australia	na	na	12.4	7.8	6.7	6.0
Belgium[a]	1.4	3.4	5.9	3.6	6.7	nil
Canada	na	4.7	11.1	5.0	2.0	0.3
France[b]	1.4	7.8	8.7	6.2	5.4	−1.2
Germany	0.8	4.1	4.7	2.6	3.4	1.5
Holland	na	na	5.7	2.1	4.8	−0.6
Italy[c]	na	na	16.8	9.6	5.9	4.1
Japan	na	3.8	6.5	0.8	2.1	1.6
Spain	na	na	na	8.7	4.2	2.2
Sweden	na	5.9	11.1	7.7	7.1	4.5
Switzerland[c]	1.4	4.7	2.1	2.0	4.3	1.5
UK	2.6	6.4	17.9	6.6	5.1	5.9
USA	1.2	4.5	9.3	3.9	5.1	4.9
EC	na	na	na	6.5	5.1	2.4
OECD	na	na	na	5.5	4.9	3.4

[a] Wholesale prices before 1980.
[b] Intermediate goods from 1975.
[c] Wholesale prices.

Source: OECD

Figure 13.3

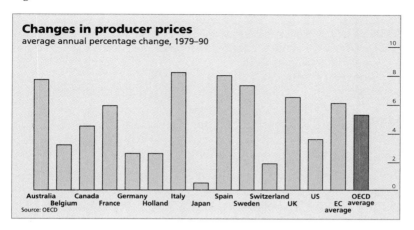

Producer input price indices vary more widely than output prices in response to movements in both commodity prices and exchange rates and are a useful guide to raw material cost pressures. See the comments on page 185 about the way that pressures feed through the system.

Seasonal adjustment. PPIs are rarely seasonally adjusted. Even if they are, the seasonal adjustment can be suspect, especially on the input side since, for example, exchange rates do not follow a neat seasonal path. Comparisons over 12 months provide a safer guide to trends, while underlying producer price pressures can often be better identified by examining PPIs excluding items such as food prices which tend to bump around erratically.

Detail. Producer price numbers are usually available at a high level of detail, covering commodity groups (metals, furniture), stages of processing (crude materials, intermediate goods) and industries (farm machinery, capital goods). Watch especially the prices of finished goods in general and of consumer goods.

Special applications. PPIs are frequently used as the basis for price indices for inflation accounting and also for contract price adjustments, often in combination with earnings indices.

197

SURVEYS OF PRICE EXPECTATIONS

Measures: Manufacturers' perceptions of inflationary pressures.
Significance: Excellent anecdotal warning of potential price changes.
Presented as: Percentage balances (for example, percentage of those expecting to raise prices).
Focus on: Trend in expectations.
Yardstick: An increase of a few points over a few months is a warning of inflationary pressures.
Released: Monthly; not revised.

Coverage and interpretation

Surveys of price expectations provide excellent inflation indicators straight from the horses' mouths. Various organisations conduct monthly or quarterly surveys (see Business conditions, page 103) in which respondents are asked questions such as: "Do you intend to raise your prices within the next four months?" The balance of those answering yes over those saying no is presented as, say, +20% or (50 + 20) = 70. If a net 20% of respondents expect to lower prices, the balance would be −20% or (50 − 20) = 30.

The absolute balance may not be a good guide, since there may always be an excess of companies planning price rises even in times of low and stable inflation. As a quick guide, see if the latest numbers are above or below figures for recent months; a change in the trend may suggest a potential increase or decrease in cost pressures. Better still, examine a long run of data so that you can put the latest figure in the context of the economic cycle.

WAGES, EARNINGS AND LABOUR COSTS

Measures: Labour costs and influences on consumers' incomes.
Significance: Indicator of both cost and demand pressures.
Presented as: Usually index form, some figures in cash terms.
Focus on: Percentage change over 12 months.
Yardstick: Compare with growth of output and consumer prices. OECD average hourly earnings in manufacturing increased by 6.0% a year during the 1980s.
Released: Mainly monthly, at least one month in arrears; revised.

Terminology

Wage rates. Basic pay per period (hour, week, and so on). Manual workers tend to have wages, white collar workers have salaries (are paid monthly).

Earnings. Basic pay plus overtime and bonuses. These may be quoted before or after tax and other deductions. Take-home pay is earnings after deductions.

Wage drift. The tendency for earnings to rise faster than wage rates, for example, due to overtime and bonuses.

Labour costs. Sometimes called total compensation, these are wages and salaries plus pension contributions, payroll taxes such as social security, free meals and a host of other perks. Non-wage costs are 20–50% of labour costs. (See also Unit labour costs, page 202.)

The Phillips curve. In the 1950s a New Zealand economist, A.W.H. Phillips, identified an apparent trade-off between unemployment and the rate of increase in wages. His curve suggested that low annual increases in wages are associated with a high unemployment rate; or, conversely, high wage inflation is associated with a low unemployment rate. (See Unemployment, page 63).

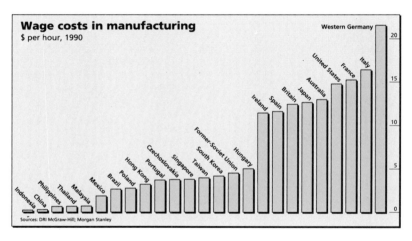

Wage costs in manufacturing
$ per hour, 1990

Sources: DRI McGraw-Hill; Morgan Stanley

WAGE COSTS

The success of the Asian NICS – Hong Kong, Singapore, South Korea and Taiwan – was based partly on their cheap labour. In 1990 manufacturing wages in the four economies (at between $3.20 and $4.16 an hour) were still only a quarter of those in America and less than a fifth of western German wages. Labour is even cheaper, however, in the newly emerging economies of Indonesia, Malaysia and Thailand, where hourly wages are less than $1. These countries are expected to see a big expansion in labour-intensive manufacturing in the 1990s. Portugal has the lowest wages of any industrial economy: at $3.69 an hour they are less than in all the NICS except Hong Kong. In 1990 they were also less than those in the former Soviet Union ($4.50).

The Economist, April 4th 1992

Key figures

Cash totals. Many government and private-sector bodies publish money wage rates and earnings in various industries, sometimes including the cash value of perks such as company cars. The figures are interesting for comparisons between industries, sectors and countries. International comparisons, however, are complicated by differences in coverage, tax regimes and by fluctuations in exchange rates.

Table 13.5   **Hourly earnings in manufacturing**
Annual % change

	1960–68	1968–73	1973–79	1979–89	1989	1990
Australia[ae]	na	na	na	7.8	6.3	5.6
Belgium	7.7	12.4	12.5	4.9	4.2	5.0
Canada	4.7	8.4	11.6	6.2	5.5	5.6
France[cd]	7.7	11.8	14.9	8.2	3.8	4.6
Germany	7.9	10.6	7.2	4.3	4.0	5.5
Holland[c]	na	na	9.4	2.9	1.4	2.9
Italy[d]	8.0	15.3	22.1	11.8	6.1	7.2
Japan[b]	11.2	17.3	11.8	4.1	5.8	5.3
Spain[f]	na	15.3	26.1	12.6	7.3	8.7
Sweden	na	na	11.1	8.4	9.9	9.4
Switzerland	5.3	7.6	4.9	4.1	3.7	na
UK[a]	na	11.5	16.6	10.1	8.8	9.4
USA	3.6	6.3	8.6	4.6	2.9	3.3
EC	na	na	12.5	8.0	7.0	6.2
OECD	na	na	na	6.0	5.2	4.9

[a] Weekly earnings.
[b] Monthly earnings.
[c] Wage rates.
[d] All industries.
[e] All non-farm industries.
[f] All non-farm, non-government.

Source: OECD

Time series. Governments also produce indices showing trends in wages and earnings, while various organisations (including those mentioned in Business conditions, page 103) track pay

Figure 13.4

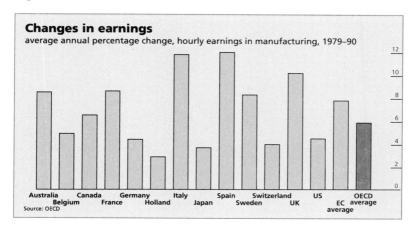

Changes in earnings
average annual percentage change, hourly earnings in manufacturing, 1979–90

Source: OECD

settlements. These are important indicators of both cost pressures and aggregate demand. Personal incomes (see page 81) offer a better guide to potential consumer demand because earnings are usually quoted before tax and other deductions, often cover only part of total employment and may ignore income from self-employment.

At one extreme, American average weekly earnings exclude salary-earners and cover only production and non-supervisory workers. At the other, British average earnings cover both manual and. non-manual employees. Other differences in coverage are highlighted by the footnotes to Table 13.5.

Interpretation

Wages and earnings are closely linked to the economic cycle. When aggregate demand begins to recover after a recession, producers respond first by increasing overtime and earnings rise faster than wage rates. Only when higher demand seems more established do employers take on more workers, which then puts upward pressure on wage rates. When the cycle turns and output begins to decline, overtime is cut first and earnings rise less rapidly or fall. Then staff are laid off. The annual increase in wage rates tends to decline as unemployment rises, though usually with a lag.

A change in average earnings can reflect changes in wage rates, total hours, the mix of standard hours and overtime, output (piecework and profit-sharing), and the relative mix of jobs, grades, industry, and so on.

In general, if earnings are rising faster than consumer price inflation, real spending power is growing. It should be noted, however, that earnings data can be distorted by industrial disputes, delays in implementing pay settlements, lump-sum back pay and temporary lay-offs during bad weather.

UNIT LABOUR COSTS

Measures: Labour costs per unit of output.
Significance: Indicator of cost pressures and competitiveness.
Presented as: Index form.
Focus on: Percentage change over 12 months.
Yardstick: OECD average unit labour costs in the business sector rose by 4.5% a year during the 1980s.
Released: At least one month after the end of the quarter; frequently revised.

Significance

Unit labour costs (ULCs) measure the average cost of producing one unit of output; for example, labour costs divided by GDP. This is a key indicator of the cost efficiency of labour. If unit labour costs fall, the same output can be produced for less expenditure on labour.

Unit labour costs reflect two factors, labour costs and productivity. Britain's appallingly rapid increases in unit labour costs in 1989 and 1990 (see Table 13.6) reflect the twin evils of rising wages and falling output, and hence declining productivity.

The cycle

Within the economic cycle, the rate of increase in unit labour costs generally peaks 12–18 months after a peak in activity. When output first begins to fall ULCs rise faster because there is less production for the same spending on labour.

Competitiveness

Relative movements in unit labour costs are important signals of international competitiveness in traded goods. A country with unit labour costs rising faster than those of its competitors might temporarily absorb the pressures by cutting profit margins or improving efficiency.

In the longer term deteriorating competitiveness will reduce exports, output and employment and so eventually tame inflation the hard way. Some economists still advocate devaluation to restore price competitiveness, but experience shows that the initial benefit is quickly eroded by faster inflation. A fixed exchange rate (as in the European Monetary System) can impose a useful discipline on pay bargaining.

Table 13.6 **Unit labour costs in the business sector**
Annual % change

	1965–73	1973–79	1979–87	1988	1989	1990
Australia[a]	7.6	13.1	7.6	7.4	8.5	8.1
Belgium[a]	7.7	9.8	4.0	−1.4	1.9	2.9
Canada[b]	3.8	8.8	5.8	5.2	5.2	6.8
France	4.3	11.4	7.1	0.9	2.0	3.2
Germany	4.6	4.3	3.0	0.1	0.4	2.3
Holland[a]	8.9	7.2	1.9	0.5	−2.0	2.7
Italy	5.2	17.4	11.7	4.2	5.8	7.6
Japan	5.4	9.2	1.2	−1.3	1.0	0.5
Spain	8.2	19.0	8.1	3.1	4.6	6.2
Sweden	4.5	11.9	6.6	7.1	9.6	10.8
Switzerland	6.2	5.1	3.8	2.6	2.8	7.2
UK	5.9	15.6	6.8	7.4	9.6	11.1
USA	4.7	8.1	4.9	3.5	2.9	4.2
EC[c]	5.5	11.4	6.5	2.7	3.7	5.6
OECD[d]	5.1	9.7	4.9	2.3	3.0	4.2

[a] 1970.
[b] 1966.
[c] Excluding Luxembourg.
[d] Excluding Iceland, Luxembourg and Turkey.

Source: OECD

CONSUMER OR RETAIL PRICES

Measures: Price of a basket of goods and services.
Significance: Indicates inflation as experienced by a "typical" household.
Presented as: Monthly index numbers.
Focus on: Percentage changes.
Yardstick: OECD average consumer prices rose 6.7% a year during the 1980s.
Released: Monthly, one month in arrears; quarterly in Australia, New Zealand and Ireland; rarely revised.

Composition

The consumer price index (CPI) is the indicator most people use to track inflation. The index is familiar and readily available, but not necessarily accurate. The British call it the retail price index (RPI), while the Germans prefer to call theirs the cost of living index.

Basket contents and weighting. RPIs measure the cost of a basket of goods and services purchased by the average household each month. The basket's composition and weighting are usually based on surveys of household or family expenditure habits.

Some indices cover "essentials" only. By careful selection a consumer price index can be dominated by subsidised commodities and those subject to official price controls. This is how some third world states keep down their reported consumer price inflation. Most indices, however, cover a fairly full range of discretionary expenditure.

Weights are updated annually in Britain and France, but most countries change their weights only every 5–10 years. Indeed, Switzerland's date from 1975 and Germany's from 1985.

Price data. Taxes on expenditure and subsidies are included in CIPs; it would be difficult to exclude them. Other taxes such as those on incomes are excluded, as are savings, life assurance premiums and capital spending.

Prices are usually found by observation, perhaps of over 100,000 items each month. Collection points vary from six state capitals in Australia to over 100 urban centres in France and Germany.

The information is collected by surveys on a particular day so a price change late one month may not be caught in the index until the following month. Indeed, in America, for example, prices of most goods and services other than food and fuel are collected monthly in the five largest geographic areas and every other month in the remaining 80 survey locations. In some other countries major surveys are conducted only every three months.

Housing. The British and Canadian indices exclude the cost of houses and capital repayments on home loans but include mortgage interest payments. As a result, if the government increases interest rates to squeeze inflationary pressures, the index rises automatically, which is exactly the opposite to the desired and underlying effect. Most other countries use a more satisfactory rental equivalent for measuring housing costs.

Variations

Many countries produce more than one CPI. America has two main indices: the CPI-U for urban consumers (about 80% of the population) and the CPI-W for wage earners (32% of the population). Britain has additional indices for pensioner households.

Britain also has a tax and price index (TPI). This was introduced in 1979 to show how VAT increases (which pushed up the RPI) were more than offset by lower income tax (which had no effect on the RPI). The idea was to dissuade workers from demanding large wage rises to keep up with the RPI. The TPI is still published, but it was quietly forgotten once it began to rise faster than the RPI.

Use and abuse

CPIs are the most timely and best understood inflation indicators. They are often used in setting wage demands and in determining index-linked pay, pension or social welfare payments. They are also used to convert wages and prices of consumer goods (including capital items such as houses) into "real" terms. The British tax authorities use the RPI to determine the allowance that can be made for inflation when calculating capital gains tax liability.

Consumer expenditure and GDP deflators are often better guides to inflation, but usually they are not available quickly enough.

Interpretation

Getting at the underlying rate of inflation may not be easy. CPIs are generally not seasonally adjusted and the necessary 12-month comparison is slow to highlight changes in trends. Looking at movements over the latest few months can be misleading because of erratic and distorting factors such as seasonal variations in food prices, annual price-cutting sales promotions, once-off changes in the rate of sales tax and erratic bumps in oil prices.

It is almost always necessary to make adjustments to highlight

Figure 13.5

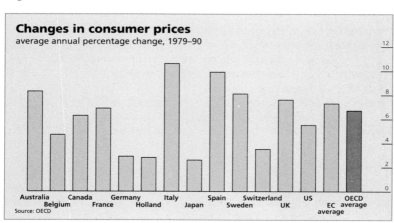

Changes in consumer prices
average annual percentage change, 1979–90

Australia Canada Germany Italy Spain Switzerland US OECD
Belgium France Holland Japan Sweden UK EC average
Source: OECD average

the "core" rate of inflation. Many statistical agencies produce helpful sub-indices, usually excluding food and energy prices. There is a tendency for such tampering to vary over time depending on short-term political requirements; the British tax and price index is a good example.

Table 13.7 **Consumer prices**
Average annual % change

	1960–68	1968–73	1973–79	1979–89	1989	1990
Australia[ae]	2.2	5.6	12.1	8.4	7.6	7.3
Belgium	2.8	4.9	8.4	4.8	3.1	3.4
Canada	2.4	4.6	9.2	6.5	5.0	4.8
France[cd]	3.6	6.1	10.7	7.3	3.6	3.4
Germany	2.7	4.6	4.7	2.9	2.8	2.7
Holland[c]	3.6	6.9	7.2	2.8	1.1	2.5
Italy[d]	4.0	5.8	16.1	11.1	6.6	6.1
Japan[b]	5.7	7.1	9.9	2.5	2.3	3.1
Spain[f]	6.6	7.1	18.3	10.2	6.8	6.7
Sweden	3.8	6.0	9.8	7.9	6.4	10.5
Switzerland	3.4	5.6	4.0	3.3	3.2	5.4
UK[a]	3.6	7.5	15.6	7.4	7.8	9.5
USA	2.0	5.0	8.5	5.5	4.8	5.4
EC	3.7	6.2	12.3	7.5	5.3	5.7
OECD	3.1	5.9	10.5	6.7	5.9	6.2

[a] Rent excluded before 1976.
[b] For households of wage and salary earners.
[c] Imputed rent excluded before 1969.

Source: OECD

CONSUMER OR PRIVATE EXPENDITURE DEFLATORS

Measures: Price changes affecting total consumers' expenditure.
Significance: A broad indicator of consumer price inflation which is less susceptible to fiddling than consumer price indices.
Presented as: Quarterly and annual index numbers.
Focus on: Percentage changes.
Yardstick: OECD average consumer expenditure deflators rose by 6.4% a year during the 1980s.
Released: Quarterly, at least one month in arrears; frequently revised.

Advantages

Consumer expenditure or private consumption deflators are derived from current and constant price estimates of total consumer expenditure. This reflects actual spending which is arguably better than the consumer prices basket approach of out-lays by an average family. It also avoids a selective approach when specifying what goes in the basket.

In addition, consumer prices data are collected at one point each month, while deflators relate to averages over the period, usually three months at a time. The deflators normally include an imputed figure for house rents, which is less distorting than the interest-rate approach used for the British RPI and the Canadian CPI.

Problems

Deflators are not available as rapidly as consumer price indices and the deflators are revised more often. Movements in implicit price deflators reflect changes in the composition of consumers' expenditure as well as changes in prices (fixed-weight deflators avoid this problem). The personal sector is broader than house-holds; it often also covers unincorporated businesses (such as farms, pension funds and trusts) and private non-profit bodies (such as charities and trade unions).

Table 13.8 **Consumer expenditure deflators**
Annual % change

	1960–68	1968–73	1973–79	1979–89	1989	1990
Australia	2.5	6.1	12.5	8.3	6.7	6.2
Belgium	3.2	4.4	8.0	4.9	3.4	3.5
Canada	2.5	4.1	8.6	6.1	4.7	4.2
France	3.8	6.4	11.1	7.4	3.4	2.9
Germany	2.7	4.6	4.6	2.9	3.1	2.6
Holland	3.8	7.0	7.2	2.8	1.6	2.4
Italy	3.8	6.7	16.8	11.2	6.2	6.3
Japan	5.6	6.8	9.4	2.2	1.8	2.7
Spain	6.2	7.3	18.1	10.3	6.6	6.4
Sweden	4.0	6.0	10.4	8.4	7.2	9.3
Switzerland	3.9	6.0	4.1	3.4	3.7	5.4
UK	3.5	7.0	15.6	7.0	5.5	6.0
USA	2.3	4.5	7.9	5.1	4.5	5.0
EC	3.2	5.9	10.4	7.1	4.5	4.4
OECD	2.9	5.3	9.0	6.4	4.4	4.7

Source: OECD

Bottom line

Consumer expenditure deflators should be used with care. They usually provide a valuable alternative to consumer price indices. If nothing else, they are a useful check on the signals from other inflation indices.

GDP DEFLATORS

Measures: Overall national price changes.
Significance: Broadest indicator of inflation.
Presented as: Quarterly and annual index numbers.
Focus on: Percentage changes.
Yardstick: OECD average GDP deflators rose by 6.0% a year during the 1980s.
Released: Quarterly, at least one month in arrears; frequently revised.

Definition

Deflators measure the difference between current and constant price GDP and its components. For example, if GDP increases by 2% in real terms and 5% in nominal terms, the implied economy-wide rate of inflation is 3%.

Table 13.9 **GDP deflators**
Annual % change

	1960–68	1968–73	1973–79	1979–89	1989	1990
Australia	2.6	6.9	12.3	8.4	7.9	4.1
Belgium	3.2	5.5	8.1	4.5	4.5	3.0
Canada	2.8	5.3	9.2	5.7	4.7	3.0
France	4.0	6.9	10.9	7.2	3.2	2.7
Germany[a]	3.1	6.3	4.8	3.0	2.6	3.4
Holland	5.0	7.8	7.4	2.6	1.6	2.9
Italy	4.3	7.5	17.1	11.6	6.0	7.5
Japan[a]	5.4	6.9	8.1	1.6	1.9	1.9
Spain	6.5	7.9	18.4	10.0	6.9	7.3
Sweden	4.2	5.9	10.6	8.0	8.0	9.2
Switzerland	4.5	6.8	3.7	3.9	4.3	5.3
UK	3.6	7.5	16.1	7.5	6.9	6.8
USA[a]	2.5	5.3	8.0	4.7	4.1	4.1
EC	3.5	6.9	10.2	7.1	4.6	5.0
OECD	3.2	6.1	8.8	6.0	4.3	4.3

[a] 1989 and 1990 figures are GNP deflators.

Source: OECD

Deflators can be found at any level of detail from one component of consumer spending or business investment right up to total GDP (see Table 13.1). They are not always published, but they can be readily calculated in index form if current and constant price data are available: for each period divide the current by the constant price data and multiply by 100.

Unless otherwise stated, most deflators are implicit price

deflators. These measure changes in the composition of GDP as well as changes in price. Fixed-weight indicators show changes in price only (see page 184).

Use

Deflators are valuable for identifying trends and obtaining advance warning of price changes in many areas.

The consumer expenditure deflator is an important alternative to the consumer prices index (see page 203). The overall GDP deflator (also known as the index of total home costs per unit of home output) is the best indicator of overall economy-wide inflation.

Since deflators cover many items and price movements self-cancel to some extent, deflators do not fluctuate as much as narrower indices such as those covering consumer prices or producer prices.

INDEX

211

EUA (European unit of account) 149
Eurocurrencies 151
environmental costs 28
equilibrium 138, 140, 144
equities 178
erratic factors 70, 74, 76, 190, 194, 205
  fluctuations 21, 22, 54
  influences 24, 127
Europe 45, 66, 89, 127, 190
  Eastern 4, 45, 49, 151, 188
  see also EC and under individual country names
exchange rates 17, 122, 125, 136, 140–58, 160,
  197
  adjustable pegs 141
  changes 50, 132
  dirty floats 141
  effective (EER) 152–3
  effects 36
  forward rates 142
  nominal 142–6
  overshooting 144
  problems 48, 194
  real 129, 154–6
  spot rates 142
  stronger and weaker 142
  turbulence 187
  what determines 143–4
  who determines 145
excise duties 73, 196
expansion 39, 51–2
  funds for 99
  future 48
  rapid 45
expectations 52, 118, 169, 178
  interest and inflation 173, 175
  price 84, 198
  sales 104
  trend in 198
expenditure 25, 31–2, 35, 40, 101–2, 202
  capital 70, 95, 113
  consumer 12, 19, 31, 68, 83–7, 89, 102, 159,
    166, 205, 206–7, 209
  consumption 111
  current 69, 70; and receipts 76
  defence and 78
  family 204
  government 48, 71, 72, 78, 181
  inflationary 167
  investment 26, 113
  measure 34
  negative 72
  non-essential 118
  patterns 41
  physical assets 92
  public 68–71, 74
  retirement 85
  short-term 89
  weekly 13, 14
exports 3, 31, 32, 110, 128–34, 139
  boosting 132, 141
  developing countries 192
  exchange-rate movements and 145
  FAS (free alongside ship) 130
  FOB (free on board) 123, 127, 130
  from former Soviet Union 193
  grossly underpriced or overpriced 141
  link to 125
  money in circulation and 41
  orders 111
  unit values (prices) 124

factor cost 34–5, 41, 74
factor substitution 49
Federal Reserve System 104, 108, 137, 165, 168
  open market committee (FOMC) 169
Financial Times 104, 150n, 174n
Finland 61, 69, 77n, 103
foreign aid 134
France 76, 77n, 106, 117, 165, 204
  bond yields 176n
  broad money 161
  capacity use 103
  exchange rates 145, 147, 150, 151
  formal intervention rates 168
  health care 86

INSEE 7
  investment and savings 91
  labour force 59
  retirement 61
  share prices 178n
  statistical publications 8, 38
  total liquidity 163
  unemployment 66
Frankfurt 170
futures 142

Gallup 89
GDFCF (gross domestic fixed capital formation)
  93
GDP (gross domestic product) 1, 3, 6, 11, 12,
  15–16, 25–57 passim, 67–79 passim, 84, 92, 93,
  102–3, 106, 109, 124–39 passim, 161
  annual demand fixed in relation to 188
  at market prices 35, 74
  current period 113
  dominant sectors 47
  future 95
  GNP relative to 136
  housing and 115
  investment figures 95
  key component 83
  most recent peaks and troughs 52–3
  nominal 41–2, 44, 83
  omissions 27–9
  real 44–6, 190
  retail sales and 118
  stockbuilding and 98
  wholesale sales and 117
  see also deflators
Germany 5–6, 63, 68, 76, 77n, 113, 117, 147,
  150, 165, 176n, 204
  Bundesbank Council 169
  central bank money stock 162
  Dutch GDP and 130
  eastern 85, 112n
  Federal Statistical Office 7, 109
  focus on GNP 26
  housing starts 116
  hyperinflation 181
  inflation 182
  international competitiveness 154
  labour force 59
  manufacturing 106
  narrow money 161
  production 105
  repo rates 168
  savings 91, 99
  shadow economy 29
  shipping costs 127
  statistical publications 8, 38
  surveys 103
  trade surpluses and deficits 132
  transfer outflows 134
  Treuhand agency 76
gifts 27
gilts 173
GNP (gross national product) 25, 26, 41, 42, 124
  relative to GDP 136
gold 137, 147, 185
  flights into 187
gold standard 140–1
Goodhart's law 165
goods
  capital 102, 106, 110, 110
  consumer 110, 197
  domestic 133
  durable 87, 106, 110, 115, 117, 184
  intermediate 196n
  net exports 121
  see also services
government 68, 69, 76
Greece 61, 195
green pound 151
Group of Seven countries 4
growth 19–22, 52, 83, 87, 128, 188
  arithmetic of 49
  faster 133
  feeble 45
  future 113
  long-term 39–40, 41, 51